FACILITY MANAGEMENT MAIN FUNCTIONS

JOHN LOK

Copyright © John Lok
All Rights Reserved.

Contents

Preface   *vii*

Prologue   *ix*

Facility Management First Main Function

  1. Facility Management Reducing Long Time Repair Expenditure   3
     Function

  2. Fm Reduces Public Transport Expenses   19

  3. The Relationship Between Facility Management And Consumer   28
     Behavior

Facility Management Second Main Function

  4. Facility Management Improving Efficiency And Service Quality   43
     Function

  5. Mtr (underground Train) Transportation Service Market Facility   59
     Management

  6. Facility Management How Influences Airport And Logistic   79
     Employee Performance

  7. Psychosocial And Medical Interventions For Mental And Physical   134
     Health Facility Management Strategy

  8. Fm And Technology How Improve Organizational Efficiency   143

Preface

Introduction

Nowadays, in construction industry aspect, many businesses began to consider facility management , they believe that any properties ought need have effective facility management system in order to help their organizations any facilities can keep long time using life. The question concerns that whether facility management can bring what real benefits to any organizations, even it can influence consumers have positive consuption emotions, when they enter the shop, can they own effective facility management protection? Can facility management bring social and economic advantages? How and why can FM bring advantages to entertainment theme park and theatre organizations?

This book divides two parts. Firstly, I shall explain what is the first main function to FM in any organizations. Whether do any organizations need facility management department? What function of benefits will bring when the organization sets up one facility management department? If the organization lacked one facility management department, what the disadvantage it will bring to influence the organization's operation? Does it has relationship between raising efficiency or improving performance and facility management department?

Organization facility managment (FM) strategy aims to keep the best facility equipment repair improvement to let any organizational equipment can be used in long time. Hence, FM aims to help organizations to avoid to spend much expenditure on long time repair. When any organizational equipment can be improved to achieve good quality. Instead of improvement equipment quality aspect, can improvement facility equipment bring good customer emotion?

I shall discuss why heatre facilities ought need to be improve in order to let audiences to feel comfortable and enjoyable to see anny performances, when audiences are sutting in any theatre halls. Hence, instead of whether theatre performers whose performance skills can atrract to satisfy audiences whose visual and listening entertainment feeling needs. Any theatre facilities ought need have attractive design feeling, comfortable seats, cleaning theatre performance hall environment to let any one theatre audience can satisfy the theatre performance in long time when they are sitting in the theatre.

The question concerns how and why theatre facilities management (CM) can being positive and negative emotion influence to any one theatre audience as well as how to improve the theatre facilities in order to attract more audiences to choose the theatre to see any performances in the theatre.I shall attempt to indicate reasons to explain how and why facility management can bring positive and negative indirect psychological relationship to influence any one audience to see any performances in any theatres.

Secondly, I shall explain what is the second main function to FM in any organizations. whether FM can help any entertainment theme park to improve any kinds of playing entertainment equipment to bring positive entertainment (leisure) playing emotion to any one theme park visitors. I shall assume that it has direct relationship between improvement entertainment theme park playing leisure facilities and theme park visitors emotions in order make conclusion concerns that how improvement leisure theme park facilities can bring advantages to playing safe entertainment facilities tangible and positive visitor emotion advantages to let readers can make reasonable analysis.

I shall indicate some evidences and causations to explain what will be occured when the organization owns one facility management department or it lacks one facility management department in its organization, such as theatre and theme park organizations. Any readers can make judgement whether in what suitations , the organization needs to set up one facility management department in order to bring advantages or waste essential human resource or raise service cost from the facility management department.In my this book, I shall attempt to explain whether facility management can bring what real benefits to our societies, business organizations and economic environment. Readers may have more clear understanding what facility management functions mean.

Prologue

Table of content
Part one Facility management first main function
Chapter 1 Facility management reducing long time repair expenditure function

Facility management brings what benefits
Facility managment brings what benefits to organizations
p.4-20
Facility management brings what benefits to economy
Facility management can reduce
maintenance service expenditure p.21-31
Facility management role in
organization p.32-42
How (FM) space moving management
can bring valued add to organizations p.43-55
Reference
Chapter 2 FM reduces public transport expenses

Predictive the choosing right
data asset and (FM) analytics
solutions to boost public
transportation service quality
The relationship between facility
management and productive
efficiency p.56-70
Chapter 3
The relationship between facility
management and consumer
behavior
Facility management brings what benefits to entertainment theme
parks p.71-85
Facility management brings what advantages to theatres
Part two facility management second main function
Chapter 4 Facility management improving efficiency and service quality

function

Facility management brings what benefits
Facility managment brings what benefits to organizatio
Facility managment brings what benefits to economy
Facility management can reduce
maintenance service expenditure
Facility management role in
organization
How (FM) space moving management
can bring valued add to organizations
    Reference

Predictive the choosing right
data asset and (FM) analytics
solutions to boost public
transportation service quality
    The relationship between facility
management and productive
efficiency
    The relationship between facility
management and consumer
behavior p.86-100

Chapter 5
MTR (UNDERGROUND TRAIN) TRANSPORTATION
SERVICE MARKET FACILITY MANAGEMENT
    ● Why MTR underground train transportation needs to
know passenger behaviour.
● Why route choice can influence passenger
● behavioural choice.
● Why trip time reliability and crowding factors
can influence MTR passenger choice.
● What is the crowding difference between
train and MTR underground train.
● How MTR can attract many passengers. p.101-116

Chapter 6

Facility management how influences airport and
logistic employee performance

● Facility management assists employees
reduce maintenance service expenditure
● Facility management role in
organization
Facility management how influences
public service transport service performance
How (FM) space moving management
brings employees efficiencies
● Predictive the choosing right
data asset and (FM) analytics
solutions to boost public
transportation service quality
● The relationship between facility
management and productive
efficiency
● The relationship between facility
management and consumer
behavior
● Facility management influences
consumer satisfactory service
feeling
● Facility management how influences
employee Psychology to raise
productive efficiency

● How to impact of workplace
management on well-being and
productivity
● Facility management technological
factor how influences workers
performance in construction industry
● How organizational facility environment
factor influences new and old employees
long term performance p.117-130

Chapter 7
    Psychosocial and medical interventions
for mental and physical health facility
management strategy

● What is the new model of healthcare facility
management
● What is the tradition facilities management
model to hospitals
● Approach to reducing costs
● The path to a solution p.131-150
Reference

Chapter 8
FM and technology how improve organizational efficiency

Human Behavioral network job brings social
economic benefits
    What does human network job mean
    Why human network job behavior may influence economy

Robots take our jobs behavioral and economy influences
    Robot job behavior brings economy influences

Intellectual human economic behaviors
What does intellectual human economic behaviors
mean ?
    The relationship between social change and human
behavior
    How human productive behavior may influence economic development

● New Zealand farmer individual wine productive behavior
● America high technological productive behavior
● China share market investing behavior
Why has any individual country have many people invest share behavior
which can influence the country's macro consumption desire?
Can technology influence human shopping behavioral change?

Why and how human behavior may influence the country's economic growth or recession?

Technology how impacts human behavior changing?

How and why employees behaviors may influence economy development?

Robots invention whether they can help organizations to raise efficiencies or inefficiencies? p.151-180

Facility management first main function

Facility management reducing long time repair expenditure function

Why do many organizations begin to feel facility management importance? What are the real functions that when one organization can attempt to achieve facility management strategy? The main functions of facility managment may include. For example, when sale manager is is directly responsible for managing the performance of salespeople, facility managment seems that it can not help any salepsople to increase sale number, they have no direct relatonship, but in fact, any salespeople must need to stay to sell any products in the shop. SO, the shop's facility environment may have indirect relationship to influence customers purchase emotion, when they enter the shop. If the shop's facility is more attractive, it may let customers to feel comfortable to stay long time in the shop.

So, facility management influences people, processes, the building and technology to be improveed better in order to achieve good job performance or sale performance both in possible. This serves many broader goals, improving efficiency, and productivity and creating a positive workplace culture, coordinating desking arrangements, managing employees, facilitating moves and spaces utilization, handling emergency planning benefits to any organizations.

Hence, the facility management function to service aspect, they may include submitting a work order request rapidly (raising efficiency) , when the shop can be designed to have more space for service staffs to contact customers , it aims to let they feel comfortable to stay in the shop, reserving space and visitors and handling emergency action planning more easily. When the shop customer service counters have have effective enquiry place facility enviroment for customers and customer service staffs in order to let they can feel comfortable to stay to enquire and answer in the shop's service counters in long time.

ON physical building improvement aspect, effective facility management many provide repair, maintenance, and building improvement, workplace , cleaning , on-and-off site property management , e.g. improving security places to avoid theft occurrence easily. Moreover, more importance is needed for facility managers to understand and use technology, workplace management system aggregate data, which drives crucial decisions about how to run the business and shape the workplace, a modern facility management building, offices , factories , shops even living houses in order to raise amart building concept comfortable feeling to let house owners, shops staffs and customers factories workers, office staffs to feel smart facility management system lay let them to feel comfortable when they are working or living in the smart building. So, amart facility management system may bring these functions: Researching IOT devices based on data collection needs, integrating IOT devies into everyday facilities processes, determining the cost, ROI and using aggregated data to better understand the workplace.

Hence, in one smart building, facility management system can collect and analyze data from networked technologies to get insights about the workplace. This fuels better decision-making on how to optimize the work environment for the people using it. For example, all smart office technology relies on data collection , access control system supports safety, when automation technological streamlines processes. And when these's a data component to any networked device or software, the true benefit of most technology is in its function. So, future smart offices , houses, factories etc. building will be needed to apply facility management technology to let any one feels comfortable when they need to use the building smart office or house or factory automatic turn off light facility when the office facility management system can help all the building all offices to turn off the light or central air condition automatically in order to save power or reduce energy waste in any office inside working environment any time when the facility management samart system ensure that none any one is staying in the building any offices.

Hence, facility management ought bring these benefits to any business office users or house living users, they may include tha complete management and maintenance of the buildings, people and assets of the business, it enables a more cost-effective working process within the business, it improves the efficiency of the business, e.g. raising workers productivities when they need to stay long time in the factory to manufacture any products, if they feel the factory environment is more comfortable and safe to let them to work, their emotion may be influenced to feel more happy to work, even raising the product manufacturing number more efficienly, it improves the efficiency of the business, it helps to manage health and safety requirements in accordance with industry requirement, helping a workplace run at maximum efficiency, e.g. cost reduces, space optimization , creating a comfortable feeling in a better workplace, outsourcing facility management service may brings better service delivery, more variety snf flexibility, today's employees and tenants expect more then just clean restrooms and adquate lighting to create and enhance great company cultures.

So, FM provides and manages a variety , it supports services in order to organize all the organization's functions more efficiently. It focuses on the integration of primary activities on both strategic and operational levels. Moreover, facilities management can be defined as the tools and services that support the functionality, safety and sustainability. For outsourcing facilty managmeent advantage., it may involve turning over the complete management and decision making authority of an operation to somebody outside organization. It may help businesses to maximize returns on investment and establish long term competitive advantage in the markplace. Hence, the types of facility management may include: cleaning, hardware inspection and maintenance, transportation, security service, fire safety. However, there are some differences between facilities management function and property management funciton. In general, facility management and office management are concerned with the people using the space, when property management concerned with the space itself only, e.g. the physical building shell and rented offices etc. buildings.

Facility management brings what benefits

Facility managment brings what benefits to organization

Can facility management bring social benefits? What benefits do facility management bring to our societies? What are social responsibilities to facility management? Why do our societies need facility managment services? I shall attempt to explain as below:

IN fact, ay organizations will need facilities management services, because it can bring continuous development benefits on economy, environment and society aspects, e.g. minimising waste to landfill form the organization, when the organization has effective facility managment service, increasing supply chain opportunities, when the organization can apply facility management skill to arrange how to let worehouse or store space can keep goods to put on corrective positions and more space to put their goods in warehouse. So goods can be transported to move more easily when the warehouse can have effective transportation to different countries more efficiently in short delivering time as well as when global warewhouses can have effective facility management service to be arranged how to store their goods in warehouses efficiently in order to bring rapid transportation benefits between the country and another country. It is significant " rapid goods transportation deliving benefit" to any organizations. For Amazon example, it needs to manage different goods to keep to its different countries warehouses in order to transport goods to fly to different countries customers' homes every day by air plane rapidly every day. If Amazon can have effective warehouse facility management strategy to manage how its different kinds of goods to be putted on its shelves in its different countries warehouses. Then, it's logistic workers won't need spedn much time to seek any goods on shelves in order to deliver their goods to fly to another country in short time efficienly. So, Amazon warehouses facilties managment service can help its organization to provide efficient delivering service.

How can facility managers satisfy the needs of customer when such needs changing so frequently to their organizations? Organizational justify theory indicates that where managers do not have resources available tomeet employee demands. The procedures used to divide what resources are available may be used to achieve satisfaction. How can facility management satisfy needs of customers when both these needs and environments in which they are operating change as frequently? How to match unpredictable space demand with supply? How to manage refurishment of out dated facilities, dealing with the competing space and service demand of different deparrments.

So, it brings this question: How can facility and accommodation management groups appease their customers in the intermediate term? SO, it seems that facility management can raise our social organizational justice benefits, such as improving service performance and raising customer satisfactory feeling for the organization's efficient service performance.

IN fact, efficient facility management strategy may help our social any organizations to earn these benefits. They may include: Influencing empllyees' perceptions fair procedural fairness in our social orgnaizations, the provision of timely feedback and effecgtive communication of the basis for decisions. So, effective facility management may help global organizational managers to know hoe to allocate new space that has become available to let employees to feel enjoyment to work in order to raise efficiencies or improve productivities. It will create any country's GDP growth when the organization can implement effective facility management strategy. Hence facility management can bring benefits to improving customer satisfactions, improving productivities and raising efficiencies. Then, our social organizations will have more social benefits, when GDP growht is caused by facility management service improvement to any global organizations.

Brochner (2003) pints out the reality that innovation in jointly FM brings benefits to organizations , developing goods and associated services in manufacturing is starting to surface, when the connection between facillity design and management is still weak, IN organizations, FM can meet organizational business need more appropriately, atract customers more are easier to manage and controp and operated more cost effectively, respond better to occupant needs.

After all, design has an effect on sales efficiency, staff, profit , capital investment, and maintenance cost(Ransley and lngram , 2001). These factors are the concern of facility management as much as they relate to the organization's core business success. Therefore, managing FM requirements during design is necessary for an organization to achieve its goals after occupancy a newly build facility.

For airport facility management case example, an effective management of the facility , aimed at successfully satisfying both the airport ownership and the passegners (air plane travellers) customers, should be based on agreement, network and strategic allience with FM functoins from other airports, they can apply outsourcing FM strategy to provide facility management service during travellers are staying in their airports, they can feel enjoyment in airport environment, then their shopping desire and again visiting the country's airport desire will be influenced to raise, when the country's airport can provide comfortable FM airport facility to let them to feel. Hence, FM can raise customer service perofrmance with firm's objective and service processes, drive performance improvement and increase client satisfaction, such as airport travelling places whehter how FM may influence travellers to stay how long time in the country's airport. It means that when the airport is more attraction, e.g. design is attration. Then , the airport can persuaded travellers to stay long time in the airport. Consequently, their shopping chance will increase in the airport.

Facility managment brings what benefits to economy

The economic benefits of FM organizational design . Evidence is growing that FM may help buildings provide financial rewards for building owners, operators and occupants. FM buildings typically have lower annual costs for energy, water, maintenance / repair, reconfiguring space because of changing needs, and other operating expenses. These reduced costs do not have to some at the expense of higher first costs, Through FM design and innovative use of high quality of materials and equipment, the first cost of FM building can be the same as or lower than that of a traditional building. Morevoer, some sustainable design features have higher first cost, but the payback period for the incremental investment often is short and the lifecycle cost typically lower than the cost of more traditional buildings. In additional to direct cost savings, FM buildings can provide owener and socieyt benefits, for example, FM building features can promote better health, comfort, well being and productivity of buildings, occupants , which can reduce levels of absenteeism and increase productivities. Moreover, FM buildings can also often owners economic benefits form lower risks, longer building lifetimes, improveed ability to attract new employees, when they feel office environment or warehouse , shop working environment are more comfortable to let they feel, when they are staying in these FM workplaces, reduced expenses for dealing with complaints, and increasing asset value.
Overall, Fm buildings also offer society as a whole economic benefits, such as reduced cost fomr air pollution , damage, avoiding landfills, wastewater treatment plant, power plants and distribution lies. So, low first cost and later repair / manintenance expense reducing or avoiding. Consequently, above of these will be FM building's long time economnic benefits, social benefits and organizational benefits to the building owner, its clients and our societies.

Facility management can reduce
maintenance service expenditure

Facility management provides a variety of non core operations and maintenance services to support any organizations' operation. For logistic organization example, it is possible to provide effective maintenance service to warehouse in order to reduce warehouse facilities to be damaged to bring to spend to buy any new equipment facilities expenditure. So, when the logistic compnay's warehouse facilities can be maintenanced to be the best quality. Then, they can be used these warehouses' machines facilities again. Their performance can assist workers to manufacture any products to keep the most efficiently an raising the best production performance in whole manufacturing process. Then, this logistic company's facility management department can bring to avoid purchase any new machine facilities expenditure spending. One to these warehouses' production machine facilities are kept in the best productin performance environment evem in long term production need.

The logistic industry's facility management department can create cost savings and efficiency of the warehouse's workplaces. It's machines facilities (producton machines) are dealt with the maintenance management of the physical assets maintenance service. FM (facilities management) has been being applied to industrial facilities in logistic and warehouse industry long term as well as maintenance plays a significant role to ensure the full service and the warehousing system, including both building components and equipment in warehouse.

Maintenance service is needed to bring a certain level of availability and reliability of a warehouse facilities system and its components and its ability perform to a standard level of quality. So , it seems that logistic industry's warehouse asset cost reducing. It depends on whether it has one facility management deparrment to provide maintenance service to itself warehouse workplace's production machine facilities and warehouse building itself in order to let workers t feel the manufacturing machines can bring good manufacturing performance to assist them to produce any products in one safe warehouse workplace environment. Hence, the performance measurement of warehouse maintenance issue will be valued to be consider to every warehouse manager and facility manager in logistic industry.

In logistic industry, (FM) works at two level on the one hand, it provides a safe and efficient working environment, which is essential to influence warehouse workers whether how they perform to do their manufacturing tasks or logistic goods delivery tasks in warehouse. When they feel the warehouse is safe environment to work. They will not need to consider anywhere has risk to cause they die by accident in warehouse. Hence, they can concentrate on doing their every tasks . On the other hand, it can involve strategic issues, such as property (warehouse workplace and management, strategy property decision and warehouse facility, e.g. manufacturing macine, facility maintenance and checking planning and maintenance planning development.

However, reducing the operating expense issue will be the main aim when the logistic company feels that it has need to set up one in-house facility management department to carry on any maintenance service for its warehouses' any workplace property and manufacturing machines facilities. So, when the logistic company decides to implement one facility management department, it needs to ensure its facility management department can bring the minimum level of keeping manufacturing performance and efficiency to its warehouses' any manufacturing machines and warehouses' property to avoid to be damaged in shourt term, such as loss of busness due to failure in service, provision of project to customer satisfaction, provision of safe environment, effective utilisation of workplace space, e.g. warehouse effectiveness and communication between the workers and the logistic managers in the warehouse workplace , due to the warehouse's space is not enough maintenance service reliability to the logistic company's warehouse, responsiveness of the warehouse's worker individual negative emotion problem, due to hs/she often feels need to work in one unsafe warehouse working environment. Hence, it seems that poor or unsafe warehouse working environment can influence workers feel negative emotion to work to bring low efficiency (inefficiency) or under productive performance in warehouse. It has relationship to influence they to bring psychological negative emotion feeling to work when the organization lacks one effective warehouse management repairing service to be provided to the warehouse's facilities and properties' maintenance needs in order to avoid ineffective measurement and misleading of performance.

Hence, the logistic company's facilities management department often needs to be reviewed whether irs maintenance service level is passed to achieve the lowest repair (maintenance) service standard to its warehouse itseld property and manufacturing machine or warehouse delivery tool facilities or warehouse lamps' light whether is enourh to let workers to see anything clearly to avoid accident occurrence or see anything to work clearly or the warehouse space areas are enough to let they can have enough space to walk or communicate to their team supervisors or deliver any goods more easily in the short distance between the worker's sending goods location and the delivering goods destination in order to avoid because the lacking enough space to cause the accident occurrence , due to the space is not enough to let they deliver their goods to any locations in warehouse.

Hence, it seems logistic company's (FM) department can contribute to the organization's mission, such as avoiding warehouse accident occurrence, inefficiency, inadequancy and unavailability of the facility for future needs when the warehouse lacks enough space areas to bring poor performance of facility and dangerous warehouse itself property in warehouse, e.g. safe and reliable operations of material handling equipment and maintenance of warehouse facilities, grounds, sesurity system, utilities, plumbing, heating , enough lightins system, air conditioning, warming heater, fire protecton, security system alarm etc. facilities in warehouse.

Hence, it seems that if the logistic company expected to reduce to spend lot of excessive manufacturing machine purchase expenditure, lossing of workers' life or bring workplace accidents , due to poor warehouse workplace environment, even bringing lawsuit compensation claim loss , due to the worker individual accident or death is caused from the poor warehouse facilities, or bring negative emotion to let the workers feel they are working in unsafe warehouse workplace environment. Then, it ought choose to set up on facility manageemtn department in order to provide enough maintenance service to its warehouse to avoid these non essential expenditure causing , due to these poor warehouse facilities factors.

Hence any logistic company ought choose to set up one itself in -house facility management department, it be better than outsourcing its all facilities service to one facility mangement (maintenance service provider) to help it to deal any kinds of maintenance service in warehouse. Because it is long term maintenace need to its warehouse's any machines and warehouse itself properties. If it chose to find one outsourcing facilitiy management maintenance service provider to replace its in-house facility mangement department to deal all related facilities maintenance tasks in warehouse. Then, it is possible that it needs to pay long time facilities maintenance service fee to its outsourcing facility management maintenance service provider more than itself facility management maintenance service provision department.

In conclusion, to decide whether the company ought need or not need facilities maintenance service or either set up in-house facility management department or outsource one facility management maintenance service provider. It depends on whether its organization has how many facilities are used in its workplace, how many staffs are working the workplace, how much size of its workplace, its workplace is office or warehouse or factory, how long time of its facilities' useful time etc. factors , then it can decide whether it needs or does not need one facility maintenance service deparment or outsouring facility maintenance service provider to help it to deal any facilities management problem in its organization.

Facility management role in
organization

When one company feels that it has need facility management service. It can choose to set up either in-house facility management department or seek one outsourcing facility management service provider to help it to arrange any facility management service need. However, this facility management role is only one for the organization. It concerns this question: What facility management maintenance function can bring the benfits to the organization?

It can define that all services required for the management of building and real estate to maintain and increase their value, the means of providing maintenance support, project management and user management during the building life cycle, the integration of multi-disciplinary activities within the built environment and the mangement of their impact upon people and the workplace. In traditional, (FM) services may include building fabric maintenance, decoratin and refurbishment, plant, plumbing and drainage maintenance, air conditioning maintenance, lift and escalator maintenance , fire safety alarm and fire fighting system maintenance, minor project management. All these are hard services. Otherwise, cleaning , security, handyman services, waste disposal, recycling, pes control, grounds maintenance, internal plants. All tese are soft services. Additional services, might also include: pace planning, things moving management, business risk assessment, business continuity planning, benchmarking, space management, facilities contract outsourcing service arrangement, information systems, telephony, travel booking facility utility management, meeting room arrangement services, catering services, vehicle fleet management, printing service, postal services, archiving , concierge services, reception services, health and safety advice, environmental management.

All of these services will be every organiztion's in-house facility soft or hard services needs. So, it explains why some large organizations feel need one effective facility management department to help them to arrange how to implement facility serivices efficiently in order to achieve cost reducing, raising efficiency and performance improvemen aims because one effective facility management control system can influence employee individual productive effort to be raised or reduced indirectly.

However, (FM) can be selected either setting up one in-house (FM) department or outsourcing its services to one facility mangement service provider to help the organizatin to solve any kinds of facilities maintance service problems. One on-house (FM) department is a team, it needs employees to deliver all (FM) services. Some specialist services are needed to be outsourced, when the service is on expertise in the company. The no expertise services will be outsourced to simple service contracts, e.g. lift and escalator (FM) department will have direct labour, but it can outsource some specialist to help it to do some complect facilities management service. So, the team leader can of can manage whose team staffs, such as maintenance technicians run low risk operations . Otherwise, the outsourcing facility management service provider needs to help it to operate high risk operations or maintenance vital plant facility management service. Anyway, it can set up in-house (FM) department to arrange specialist direct labour and outsourced (FM) services to more than one facility management service providers to do different kinds of (FM) services. One of these outsourcing (FM) service provider, who can arrange sub-contractors to assist it to finish any (FM) services of it's outsourcing (FM) services are more complex to compare the other sub-contractors (third parties).

● What is a facility manager's role to provide quality service to satisfy its user needs?

We need to know how quality can be defined in facility management and why it should be defined by the customer? How facility managers can find out customer (user) needs? What are the difficulties in finding out users' needs and in delivering quality services? Whether improving quality always means requiring higher cost?

In general, facility manager's major responsibilities may include these major functional areas: longer range and annual facility planning, facility financial forecasting, real estate acquisiton and/or disposal, work specification, installation and space management, architectural and engineering planning and design, new construction and/or renovation, maintenance and operations management, maintenance and operation management, telecommunications integration, security and general administrative services. When the facility manager had implemented any one of these FM services for those user. How does he/she provide excellent (FM) service quality ot let whose users to feel satisfactory?

In fact, quality issues can not be considered without customer-oriented perspective service quality involves a comparision of expectation with performance. (FM) service quality is a measure of how well to service level delivered matches customer expectation. So, these issues are (FM) service user's general measurement level requirement. The (FM) manager needs to achieve these the minimum performance measurement level to satisfy whose (FM) user's needs.

However, (FM) service quality has three characteristics: Intangibility, heterogeneity, inseparability. But in fact, (FM) service delivered may be through tangible physical aspects, e.g. factory plant workplace building, machine equipment maintenance, intangible (FM) services, e.g. managing space moving in plant to let staffs to work, managing outsourcing cleaners to clean factory equipment. However, all (FM) service performance often varies, due to the behavior of service personnel. Hence, a well developed job specification and training can help to improve the consistence of services of (FM). Any (FM) productin and consumption of many services may are inseparable and they are ususally interactions between the (FM) client and the contact person from the service provider.

Hence, it seems that service quality is considered as hard to evaluate. In (FM) service quality, it includes physical quality and interactive non-physical service quality. Physical quality is tangibles: The appearance of the physical facilities, equipment, personnel and communication materials. Non-physical services quality means reliability: The ability to perform the promised service dependably and accurately; responsiveness means the willingness to help customers and provide prompot service to let user to feel; assurance mans the competence of the system in its credibility in providing a courteous and secure service and empathy means the approachability, ease of access and effort taken to understand customers' needs.

Hence, a good performance of (FM) manager , he/she ought satisfy the user's tangible and non-tangible both service quality needs. I recommend that he/she can attempt to predict what are the (FM) customer expects in each (FM) service needs. Then, it can make decision what aspect(s) will be the (FM) users major (FM) service need and what aspect(S) won't be the (FM) users major (FM) service need. Then, he/she can make more accurate decision to arrange time, human resource , cost spending amount arrangement whether when it ought concentrate on finishing the (FM) major service tasks as well as whether how he/she ought finish the major (FM) service tasks to be more easily, e.g. how to arrange staffs number to finish, how many the minimum staffs number is needed to be arrange the major (FM) service tasks, time arrangement is important factor, because it can influence whether he/she ought finish the major (FM) service tasks today or tomorrow or later in order to have enough time to finish other non-major (FM) service tasks. Instead of time management, staff number arrangement is also important factor , if he/she arrangeed the excessive staffs number to do the (FM) major services tasks, then it is possible that it will have shortage of staffs number to finish the non-major (FM) service tasks on the day. So, avoiding either majoe or non-major (FM) services can not finish on the day. The (FM) manager needs to predict when the major (FM) services and the non-major (FM) services which are necessary to be finished in order to have enough time and staffs to assist him/her to finish every day major and non-major (FM) servie effectively. Then, the achievement of his/her (FM) major and non-major tangible and non-tangible services , it will have more chance to be performed efficiently by his/her managed staffs.

In conclusion, in any organizations , (FM) manager needs have good predictable effort to evaluate whether when his/her managed team need to finish the major and/or non-major (FM) tasks as well as whether how he/she ought arrange the accurate time and staff number to finish any major and/or non-major (FM) service tasks on the day. Then, his/her leading of (FM) service team can be managed to work more efficiently in order to satisfy her/his (FM) service user's needs.

How (FM) space moving management
can bring valued add to organizations

There are interesting questions: How (FM) can bring value-add to avoid loss or earn more profit to the organization? Can it influence employees to raise performance and improve efficiency ? Some organizations' (FM) service need which is necessary in order to let employees can raise productivity.

It is based on these assumptions: I assume the organizations have completely either outsourced or in-house their (FM) facility management departments will gain more effect on added value than they have no (FM) function as well as organizations have a strong coordination with the (FM) department will gain more added value than organizations with a weak coordination. Organizations in the profit aim can gain more added value than organizations in the not for profit aim sectors.

In fact, any organization is difficult to confirm it has relationship between improving performance, raising efficiency and owning (FM) function in its organization. (FM) could have to do with the attraction of easy but incomplete indicators of efficiency rather than the necessarily and less direct measures if the effectiveness and the relevance of space moving useful management, e.g. whether building has the enough space to let employees to move to work easy in order to raise efficiency, whether the building has excessive furniture and equipment number and they are putted on wrong places to be caused employees move difficulty in the building in order to influence productive performance.

However, how to arrange space moving management to equipment, e.g. copying machines, faxes, productive machines, they are putted on the locations where have enough space to let employees to move to another locations. For example, the building floor has more than 50 employees, but its space is not enough to let these 50 employees to move to any locations to let them to feel easily often. Then, it is posible to cause they feel nervous pressure and they can feel difficult to work , when they are working in a small office space or factory space or warehouse space. Then, the consequence will be under-predictive efficiency or poor performance to any one of these 50 employees in this office or factory or warehouse.

" Facility management is responsible for coordinating all efforts related to planning, designing, and managing buildings and their systems, equipment, and furniture to enhance. The organizations abilty to compete successfully in a rapidly changing world." (F.Becker)

The author explains equipment, workplace internal space designing, furniture space putting location arrangement will have possible to influence employee individual productive performance or efficiency to be raised or reduced in the workplace. Hence, it seems that, in the value chain (FM) belongs to the activity part of the firm. To make the facilities cooperation with each office or factory or warehouse using space moving facility management. Facility space moving management must be linked strategically, tactically and operationally to other support activity to add value to the organization's office or factory or warehouse space moving management arrangement more effectively.

Thus, how to arrangement space moving management issue it will have possible to influence the organization's employee individual productive performance and efficiency in whose workplace. It seems that (FM) space moving management arrangement have indirect relationship to influence the organization's employee individual performance and efficiency , due to they need often to work in the workplace, if they feel moving difficulty , or excessive equipment , furniture number is putting into the small office, factory or warehouse locations, or they feel the office or factory or warehouse has excessive (a lot of) staffs number to work in the small space of office or factory or warehouse. Then, they can not concentrate nervous on finishing every tasks in possible. In long term, their efficiencies will be poor or inefficiencies or their performance won't be improved or causing poort performance in possible.

Instead of the not enough space moving and excessive staffs number factor, it will bring another question: Can enough information systems equipment cause a more efficient and improvéd performance to the organization staffs in the workplace?

I assume that the office has 100 employees and it has only ten copying machines. So it means that ten employees use one copying machine. Hence, it brings this question: Is it enough to provide only ten copying machines to average ten employees to use? It depends on other factors, e.g. whether any one of these 100 employees needs to print how many documents per day , whether the five copying machines' locations are far away to separate different locations or they are stored in one printing room in the office, whether the day has how many staffs are absent, whether the day has how many printing machine(s) is/ are broken to need to be repaired. Hence, these unpredictable external environment factors will influence whether the five copying machines number is enough to let these 100 employees to use in the office every day. Hence, facility manager ought need to spend to observe average their copying behaviors every day in order to make data record. Many employees need to use copy machines to print documents, average how many document's page number, they need to print, how much average time spending to print their documents, average how many staff absent number on the day. Even, if the all five copying machines are stored in the printing room, calculating the staffs number whether how many staffs need more than five minutes to walk to the printing room to print their documents many staffs need to spend five minute to walk to the printing room, and they have other urgent tasks to wait to finish. It is possible to influence their efficiency, due to they often need to spend more than five minutes to walk to the printing room to print documents. If there are many staffs need to often to print documents, but their printing task will have many time, e.g. 20 separate printing tasks. Then, they need to spend at least (20x5) 100 minutes to spend time to walk to the printing room to print their documents. It must influence that they should not finish the other urgent tasks on the day. If there are many staffs to spend much time to walk to the printing room in the least 20 separate printing time or more on that day. All the facility manager needs to evaluate whether all the five copy machines are stored in the printing room whether it is the best location decision or they ought need be separated to put on different office locations in their workplaces, even he/she ought need to evaluate whether it is enough copying machines number, when the office has only 5 copying machines. He/she ought need to buy more copying machines number to satisfy any one of these 100 employee individual copyiing task need.

In conclusion, effective office or factory or warehouse space moving facility management will be one part task of (FM) function. If the office or factory or warehouse can have accurate equipment, machine , furniture number to avoid excessive or shortage number problem to cause employees often feel moving difficult problem in their workplace when they need to move to another location to work in office or warehouse or factory as well as whether the staff needs often spend time to wait the another employee to use the copying machine to print whose document or fax machine to deliver whose document. Then, it is not that fax or printing machines number is not enough to provide the employees to use in the office or warehouse or factory workplace.

Hence, (FM) includes space moving facility management to equipment , machines, furniture number as well as choosing anywhere is(are) the suitable location (s) arrangement to putting or storing these facilities in workplace as well as decision of the staff number and the workplace area size whether it has excessive staffs number to cause these staffs need to work in the small area size of office or warehouse or factory workplace. So, the organization ought need to decide whether it needs to reduce the office's staffs number to let them to work in another more suitable locations in another workplace. Hence, all these facilities space moving management and staffs and workplace size issues will be (FM) manager's consideration issues, because these external environment factors will influence employee individual efficiency and performance to be ppor to cause low valued to its organization in long term in possible .

Reference

Becker, F. (1990). " Facility management : a cutting edge field?" property management 8 (2): 25-28.

CHAPTER II

FM reduces public transport expenses

Predictive the choosing right
data asset and (FM) analytics
solutions to boost public
transportation service quality

Can gather the choosing right data public transportation service station facilities asset and analytics, it can give recommendation to help any organizatin to boost service quality? (FM) analytics data can be applied to public transportation service industry to be supported how and why the train, train, ferry , ship, air plane, underground train public transportation tools' time arrival and leaving information notice board and automated ticket paying machines facilities are putting on or stored any where locations in order to boost passengers to feel their facilities locations are convenient to let them to buy tickets and see the arrival and leaving time for the next public transportation tool from the information notice electronic board machine. So, it seems that these public transportation tools' station facilities locations can influence passengers to feel the public transportation service company how to consider to its passenger's buying ticket needs and next public transporation tool's arrival and leaving time information needs in order to boost its passenges use service quality and let them to feel better service reliable performance in any train, tram, ferry , ship, underground tram, airplane stations.

As these public transportation service organizations need to learn data analytics represent an opportunity for its ticket paying machine equipment facilities as well as the next transportation tool arrival and leaving time information notice board electronic equipment facilities anywhere the locations are the most suitable to put on or store these equipment to let passengers to walk to the ticket paying machines to buy the ticket to catch the train, tram, underground train, ferry, airplane, taxt, ship more easily. So, they do not need to spend more time to find these facilities locations and spend more time to queue to wait to buy ticket to catch the public transportation tool in stations conveniently. Instead of where is the seeking ticket paying machine location, where is the next public transportation tool arrival and leaving information notice time , these both issues will be any public transportion tool's passenger's main needs.

Hence, how to spend time to seek where the next public transportation tool's arrival and leaving time information electronic notice machine location and where the ticket paying machine location , these both factors will influence any passengers' positive or negative emotion causing. For example, if the passenger feels diffcult to find the ticket paying machine in the large area size train station or /and he/she feels difficult to find the train time arrival and leaving information to let him/her to know when the next train will arrive the station. Due to he/she feels difficult to find the train ticket paying machine, he/she needs to spend much time to find any one tickeet paying machine in the train station. Then, it will influence him/her to choose another public transportation tool to replace the train public transportation tool, e.g. he/she can choose to catch tram, underground train, taxi, bus, ferry, taxi, ship to replace train. So, it seems ticket paying machine and time arrival and leaving information notice electronic equipment 's location putting or stored choice will be one factor to influence the passenger to choose another kind of public transportation tool to replace train at the moment. When, he/she feels that he/she arrives the destination in the most short time. Then, the public transportation service organization (FM) manager has responsibility to evaluate whether there are enough ticket paying machines number to let passengers do not need to spend more time to queue to buy tickets to catch the public transporation tool in short time as well as there are enough time arrival and leaving for next transportation tool to let passengers to know. It will be their concerning issues when they arrive the public transportation service tool's station.

Hence, predictive passenger individual walking behavior can help the public transportation service organization to choose whether where are the most convenient and attractive locations to let the ticket paying machines and the arrival and leaving time information electronic board machines to be putted on or stored in the suitable station positions in order to let many passengers can find these essential facilities in stations very easily. So, gathering data concerns passenger walking behavior in the public transporation service any stations, which can help the facility manager to make more accurate evaluation to attempt to predict whether where the locations are common places to let passengers to choose to walk daily or where the locations are not common places to let passenger to choose not to walk daily in general. Then, he/she can apply these data of different locations in the stations to evaluate whether anywhere they will have many passengers to choose to walk or whether anywhere they won't have many passengers to choose to walk in order to make more accurate decision whether anywhere are the most suitable locations to let the ticket paying machines and the time arrival and leaving information electronic board equipment to be putter on or stored in order to let them to feel it is so easier to let them to find.

Anyway, calculating each station's passenger number per day issue is important to predict whether where , there are many passengers choose to walk or where, there are not many passengers choose to walk in these different public transportation service stations in order to evaluate whether where the stations' different ought put on paying ticket machines or time arrival and leaving information electronic boards in order to let they feel very easy to buy tickets and seeing the next arrival and leaving time information for the kind of public transportation service tool conveniently in the different stations. Moreover, if the station has no enough ticket paying machines number to be supplied to let passengers need to spend more than ten minute time to wait to buy ticket to catch the kind of public transportation service tool in every queue every day. Then it will cause them to choose another kind of public transportation tool to catch go to working place or entertainment place to replace it to on that day. Then, it will cause these passengers who often do not like to queue in the kind of public transportation service tool's any stations, who will not choose to go to anywhere of this kind of public transportation service tool's any stations again. Hence, in long term this kind of public tranportation service tool will lose many passengers. Thus, calculating each station's busy time of passengers number , which can predict when it is the busy time and it can make more accurate decision whether the station has need to increase enough ticket paying machines number in order to bring enough supply number to satisfy passengers' ticket purchase need in the busy time.

In conclusion, gathering above all stations' public transportation service equipment facilities number, storing positions datas and every station's passenger walking behavior datas, they are necessary to any public transportation tool service industry, because these equipments' number and storing locations will influence them to make decisions to choose another kind of public transportation tool to replace it's transportation service if they often feel difficult to find these facilities in its different stations. Thus, it is part of task to facility manager's responsibility if the public transportation service organization expects it won't lose many passengers , due to these external environment factor influence and it also implies cheap ticket price does not guarantee the passengers will choose to catch this kind of public tranportation service tool to go to anywhere.

The relationship between facility management and productive efficiency

It is one interesting question: Can facility management function bring benefits to raise productive efficiency to organizations? I shall indicate some cases to attempt to explain this possible occurrence chance as below:

● Facility management benefit to office workplace

In private organizations, when the firm has facility management department, whether it can bring efficient administration to influence clerks to work efficiently in office, e.g. reducing administrative time or shortern time to work in administrative processes, in order to achieve minimizing clerk number labor cost. How to design office facilities to let office staffs to feel comfortable to work and reducing their pressure to work. It seems that office working environment will influence office staff individual performance. If the office workin environment could improve efficiency and creativity of services to satisfy office workers' comfortable working environment needs. It will reduce every administration manager's working pressuse when he/she needs often to find methods to attempt to encourage whose administrative clerks to avoid to waste working time to do some non-major administration tasks.

Hence, how to design or allocate or arrange office any facilities' stored locations or whether how many equipment number is the enough to store in the locations, which will influence office employees' working attitude in order to raise or reduce their administration tasks efficiency indirectly, e.g. the office is clean or dirty, whether office reception has enough information telephone switchboard operation facilities, whether every clerk's table has enough computers number to supply to every to use, whether internet speed is fast or slow in order to let any employees can send and receive email to communicate or download any document from internet in short time, whether data processing and computer system maintenance service supply is enough to be repaired to employees' computers immediately when their computers are broken to wait repaire, whether website editing facilties operation whether is enough to link to office every staffs in order to let any office staffs can apply internet to do their tasks conveniently in short time.

Hence, all of these general office equipment facilities whether they are enough supplied and their stored positions anywhere are the suitable to assist any clerks to work conveniently, they will influence every office employee's administrative and productive efficiency indirectly as well as all faxs, copying machines, computers, whether internet linking maintenance service time is short or long to prepare to any office employees to use conveniently any time, these different issues will also influence every employee individual efficiency in office. Hence, it concludes that office working environment, facilities supply number, facilities maintenance service and facilities location storing both factors will influence employee individual administrative productive efficieny in office.

● facility management benefits to service working environment

Can effective facility management improve service working environment to raise employee individual work performance? It is a concern about the quality of service to its customer question. The term" standards and goals" are often used to measure staff individual service performance whether he/she can serve to customers to let them to feel this staff's service performance or attitude is good or bad.

Is the service workplace working environment facilities enough, it will influence customer service staff individual performance.

For shopping center service industry case example, for this suitation, e.g. shopping center's facilities are enough or are placed to the suitable locations in order to let the shopping center's customers to feel comfortable to shopping when they enter this shopping center as well as whether the shopping center's facilities can influence the customer service staffs to serve whose shopping customers easily or difficult, due to whether the shopping center's facilities whether are adequate supplied or their locations are the best suitable positions to influence their service performance to let them to feel easier or comfortable to serve their customers in any large size shopping centers. For example, whether the lamps' lighting energy is enough to let the shoppers to feel safe to walk to visit any shops when there are many shoppers were walking to cause crowd and they feel diffuclt to walk to avoid any body contact to any one in busy time when the shopping center has no enough lights to let them to see anywhere in the shopping center's dark environment. Then it will influence customer service staffs to feel difficult to find any shopping center customers, e.g. when two shopping center customers are fighting in one location where is far away to the shopping customer service staffs and securities in the shopping center, because the shopping center is large and it has no enough light to let the customer service staffs and securities to find their frighting location to deal their fighing behavior and other shopping center's shoppers will feel very dangerous to walk their fighting location to avoid to close them. Then, it will has possible to cause death or hurt to any one of these two fighting shoppers ,even other shoppers' lifes. Because the shopping center's securities and customer service staffs who need to spend much time to find their fighting location, it will delay they can bring the policemen to their fighting location when they arrive this shopping center's destination in short time in order to solve their fighting behavior to influence all shoppers' lifes in this shopping center. Hence, the shopping center whether it has enough lamps number and the lamps' light whether is enough, these lighting facilities will influence any shopping center customer service staffs and securities who can spend less time to arrive any locations to deal any urgent matters.

For another suitation in shopping center, if the shopping center has no enough paying telephone service facilities to supply shoppers to phone to anyone when they feel need to phone to any in the shopping center. Then, it will lead to some shoppers decide to find where the shopping center's receiption's telephone to supply to them to phone call to anyone. If ther are ten shoppers are waiting to use the shopping center's receiption's telephone to phone call to their friend or family within one minute. Thus, it will influence the reception customer service staffs feel difficult to arrange how to distribute the only one telephone to these ten shoppers to use to phone call their friend or family when they are queuing within their one minute waiting time in the shopping center's reception. If these ten shoppers can not use the receiption telephone to phone call anyone. hen, they will feel disatisfactory and complain to the reception service staffs unpolitely. So, lacking enough facilities in the shopping center's any where, it will possible to influence their shopping centers' shoppers to feel all shopping center's service staff individual performance to be poor. It means that if the shopping center expects to improve customer satisfaction to its customer service staff's behavioral performance, it meets have enough facilities to be supplied in the shopping center to let its shoppers to feel it is one comfortable and safe shopping center. In conclusion, shopping center's facilities will have possible to influence shoppers' feeling to evaluate its customer service staffs to evaluate whether their service attitudes are good or poor indirectly.

● Can facility management improve productivity

The productivity means resources (input) is therefore the amount of products or services (output), which is produced by them. Hence, higher (improved) productivity means that more is produced with the same expectton of resource, i.e. at the same cost is terms of land materials, machine, time or labor. Alternatively, it means same amount is produced at less labor cost in term sof land, material, machine, time for labor that is utilized. So, it brings this question: How can facility management improve productivity? I shall explain as these several aspects, it is possible to be improved productivity from (FM) successfully.

Improved productivity of farm land: If the farming land has better facility management to bring advantages by using better seed, better facilities of cultivation and most fertilizer. It is in the agricultural sense is increased (improved). So, facility management can bring benefits to any land resource to raise productivity in possible. It implies that the productivity of land used for better facility management of industrial purposes is said to have been increased if the output of products or service within that area of industrial land is increased output aim.

Improved productivity of material: If the factory has improved better equipment by facility management method to assist skillful workers to raise the manufacture cloth number, then the productivity of the cloth number is improved by (FM) method.

Improved productivity of labour: When the factory has good manufacturing equipment facilities to be supplied to improve methods of work to product more producing number per hour, then (FM) improved productivity of worker. Hence, in any workplaces, when organization has good facilities, it will influence employees to raise productivities in possible, because they need often to improved equipment facilties manufacture products to achieve higher producton number aim.

● Can facility management raise bank employee productivity

Bank workplace environment is busy, the bank counter service staffs need to contact many bank clients to help them to serve or withdraw money from bank's counters. Whether does the quality of environment in bank workpace will influence the determination level of employee's motivation, subsequent performance productivity in bank working environment. For example, if the bnk's staffs need work under inconvenient conditions , it will bring low performance and face occupatinal health diseases causing high abenteeism and turnover.

In general, bank size is usually small, it will have many bank clients enter bank to contact counter staffs to need them to help them to save or withdraw money. So, it will bring air pollution the crowd queue in every bank counter challenge when the bank has many people are queue waiting in counters to queue. So, bank working condition problem relates to environmental and physical factors which will influence every bank counter staff individual working performance to serve bank clients satisfactory. However, bank staffs need to deal many documents concern every client personal data every day. So, they need to spend much time to use computer and painting machines. This is particularly true for these employees who spend most of the day operating a computer terminal in bank workplace. As more and more computers are being installed in workplaces, an increasing number of business has been adopting designs for bank offices installment. So, bank needs have effective facilities management design because of demand of bank staffs for more human comfort.

An good equipment facility management for bank staffs to use conveniently, it is assumed that better workplace environment can motives bank employees and produces better productivity. Hence, bank office environment can be described in terms of physical and behavioral components to influence bank staffs to work inefficiently. To achieve high level of abnk employee productivity, bank organizations must ensure that the physical environment in conductive to bank different department organizational needs, facilitating interaction and privacy, formality and informality, functionalit and disciplinarily, e.g. house loan or private loan departmets, counter service department, visa card application department. Thus, in a high safe privary facility management working environment will let different department bank staffs feel safe to worry about privacy loss in possible. So, the improving bank facility to bring safe and high privacy to avoid bank client individual loss in working environment issue, the facility management can be results to bring these benefits, such as in a reduction in a number of complaints and absenteeism and an increase in productivity.

● Can (FM) create value to organization?

(FM) can reduce managing facilties as a strategic resource to add value to the organization and its overall performance, e.g. saving the energy in building and take care of shuttle buses and parking facilities space management for brikes, on economic efficiency and effectiveness, or good price and value for the organization.

If the organization expects to apply (FM) process to save energy, it depends on possible input factors, i.e. interventions in the accommodation facilities services. So, it seems that the organization expects to save its energy consumption in its building. It needs have goos space management facilities between parking its shuttle buses and brikes in its property's car park.

Why does space facility management is important to influence efficiency and productivity. For one school's building example, when the school decides none of the two gymnasiums student sport entertainment centers to be built in order to reduce financial cost and higher benefits. Remarkably, the use of space with the school overall strategic goals , such as creating spaces that better can support the teaching, motivate students and teachers, attract more students and increase the utilisation of existing space to accomodate an increasing number of students.

If it hopes to make high quality teaching facilities on student's choice where to study. The school will need to choose to build either one comfortable and new design facility teaching accommodation or build two gymnasium sport entertainment centers in its limited land space either for students' learning or sport aim. Due to it feels new teaching accommodcation can make more attractive to increase students numbers to choose it to study more than building two new gymnasusm sport centers to let them do sport in school. Hence, space choise (FC) management strategy will be one important considerable issue, when the organization has limited land space resources to make choose to build any constructions in order to increase many clients number. Such as the school organization has limited stortage land resource to let it to build either two gymnasium sport entertainment centers or one new teaching accommodation in order to attract many students to choose it to learn. Hence, it needs to gather data to make more accurate evaluation to decide how to apply its space facility to choose to build these both kinds of buildings in order to achieve the attractive student learning choice aim, so whether teh two sport entertainment activity centers or one new teaching accommodation choice, it needs to gater information to decide whether the school ought to choose to build which kind of building in order to achieve the increase of student number aim, so space facility management will be this school's land shortage problem.

The relationship between facility management and consumer behavior

How and why shop facility management can influence consumer individual shopping behavior? If it is possible, what shop facility management factors can influence their consumption decision when they enter the shop to plan to buy anything. I shall indicate some shop case studied to expline whether how and why every shop's facility management can influence consumer individual consumption desire when any one consumer enters any shops.

● Shop's low ceiling height location (FM) influcence consumer behavior

Can the shop's ceiling height influence shoppers' shopping behavior? Can the shops's variation in ceiling height can influence how consumers process information to decide to make purchase decision in the shops, e.g. for this suitation, when the consumer enters the shop, he/she feels the ceiling height is low and it has a lamp wil contact his/her head in possible. So, he/she chooses to move far away from the low ceiling beight location in the shop. It is possible that shop's ceiling low height and the lamp locates at the ceiling low height position will influence many customers' choices to leave the low ceiling height and lamp location, then the shop's low ceiling height will have possible to influenced many customers to choose to find the another shop to buy the similar kind of products , due to the lamp locates in the low ceiling height, so this lamp and low ceiling height will be possible factor to influence any shoppers who won't choose to walk to this dangerous location in the shop. If the shop's all spaces are ceiling height and it has many lamps are located at the low ceiling height spaces. Then, it will be serious to cause many shoppers do not want to spend too much time to choose any products in the shop because they feel dangerous to walk to the any low ceiling height lamps' locations in the shop.

Hence, hoe to design the different concept may be activated by the showroom ceiling if it were relatively high, as it tends to be in mall stores, versus low, as it is in most strip mall shops and outlet centers. Relatively high ceilings may bring safe shopping emotion to let any consumers to feel thoughts related to freedom, whereas lower ceilings may let consumers to feel dangerous to walk the locations in any shops. Hence it seems any shops ought not neglect whether their ceiling height is tall and the lamps ought avoid to locate in any low ceiling height locations in order to influence consumers number to be decreased.

● Can house facility management influence consumer individual purchase intention?

When one new property is built, whether the property consumers will consider how the new property is facilited to influence their purchase intention to the property will the new property's (FM) influence buyers in real estate markets' preferences choice and living interest. Any new property's internal characteristics of the house unit itsel , such as rooms available, when example, of external are location, accessibility to utilities services and facilities will have possible to influence the property buyer's final property purchase decision, so it seems that even the property price is cheap, it is not represent the property buyer will choose to buy the property, if he/she feels the property's facility mangement is poorer to compare other similar kinds of properties.

So, it can help real estate analysts better explain and predict the behavior of decision makers in real estate markets. Property consumers will search for property information, concerns the property's quality, price distinctiveness, ability, facility mangement, service of the property's external environment to decide whether the property is high value to choose to buy to compare other kinds of properties.

However, the external environmental forces, such as limited resources, e.g. time or financial will influence whose property consumption choice and living the property's satisfaction feeling (represent) a feedback machanism from post-property purchase reflection used to inform subsequent decisions. The process of the property buyer's leaving experience will serve to influence the extent to which the property consumer how to consider future next time property purchases decision and new information methods. Hence, when one property consumer chooses to buy a house, it refers house features ar house internal attributes , such as quality of building, the design as well as internal and external design, which are important factors for a property consumer when he/she needs to select and purchases one house.

The other (FM) factors which can influence the property consumers' needs, include living space as features, such as the size of kitchen, bathroom, bedroom, living bath and other rooms available in the house. The environment of housing area is also important factor, e.g. the condition of the neighbourhood, attractiveness of the area, quality of neighbouring houses, type of neighbouring houses, type of neighbouring houses, density of housing, wooded area or free coverage, slope of the attractive views, open space, non-residential uses in the areas vacant sites, traffic noise, level of owner-occupation in neighbourhoos, level of education in neighbourhood level of income in neighbourhood, security from crime, quality of schools, religious of neighbourhood, transportation , shopping center, sport entertainment can be supplied to close to the house area. All these human related issue of the property's location will also influence the property buyer's living location selection. Hence, above (FM) influence property consumer purchase behavior, it is based on the relationship behavior. The consumer's house purchase intention and house features, living space, environment and distance to recreation center, supermarket, library etc. public facilities variable (FM) factors.

In conclusion, the house internal space facility management and external environment facility management factors will influence property consumer individual house purchase intention.

● The effects of in-store shelf design facility management factor influences consumer behavior

Can every store retailer's shelf design influence supermarket and large retail stores shoppers' behaviors when they visit the stores? However, currently many stores tend to build on traditional and repetitive design for their store shelf layout, it brings results in outdated store layouts.

Another important store shelf layout design aspect, retailer should consider carefully is the allocation of products on shelves. So, it seems that efficienct shelf space allocation management does not only minimize the economic threats of empty product shelves, it can also lead to higher consumer satisfaction, a better customer relationship.

Why does supermarket shelves design is important? Any retail tore will sell product category within a shelf. They can use the same nominal category , e.g. negular crisps next to light crisps, same food prouct shelf. Anyway, a goal-based shelf display can contain several product, that determine a common consumer goal, e.g. fair trade. Hence, these two categorical product structuring methods are also described in terms of how to put product, or food on shelf benefit and attribute -based product categories.

These shelf design food or product storing method will have more influence consumers to choose to buy the supermarket or retail store food or products more easily , due to products, or food put on their shelf very convenient and systematic to attract consumers' shopping consideration to the supemarket or retail store.

● Music (FM) environment influence consumer consumption desire

Is it possible that shop music (FM) environment can raise consumer purchase desire? In one shop or supermarket, it can provide soft music (FM) equipment to let consumers can listen soft music or songs in the supermarket or retail shop when the are staying to spend more time shopping and whether soft music facility can be expected to raise customer individual value-added options to the music facility shop in the supermarket ot retail shop.

Can the music facilities prolong consumers to stay in the store? It is possible that tempo soft music can influence consumers to stay longer time in restaurants and supermarkets and retail shops. It is possible that the different types of music (FM) in any supemarket, restaurant, retail shop owning music listening facility shopping environment. It will have possible to influence consumers to prolong staying in their shops. For example, one wine selling retail shop has classical music (FM) listening equipment to let consumers to listen when they enter the wine shop, it is possible to cause consumers to choose to buy more expensive wine products. Some researchers indicate when the wine shop owns classical music facility to let all consumers can list classical music when they walk in the wine ship, it can evoke the wine consumers to choose to buy purchasing higher prices wine products in the long term classical music listening environment. Otherwise, in a fitness sport center, musical fir and excite or popular music (FM) environment can attract fitness sport players' emotion to play and kind of fitness sport facility longer time. Also, in one supermarket, the soft music facilities listening environment can persuade or attract food consumers to spend more time in the mall consuming food or beverage also purchase othe products more easily, due to they will listen soft music to be influenced to choose to prolong staying time in the supermarket. It seems that it has relationship between retail shop's music facility environment and consumer's emotion will be influenced by these different kinds of soft music or songs to raise consumption desire in the supermarket, if some consumers like to proplong to stay longer consuming time in the owning music facility environment's retail shop.

In fact, some researchers indicate the owning background music facility selling environment's ship , it can affect consumer decision making, memory, concentration consumption desire. So, classical , jazz soft music facility ought be installed in restaurants, retail shops, restaurants' environment. Otherwise, popular , exciting, noise, pop music facilty ought be installed in fitness sport centers, theme park entertainment parks business places in order to influence fitness sport players or theme park entertainers to prolong playing or entertaining time to feel real sport or entertainment theme park playing machine facility's entertainment enjoyable feeling as well as attracting restaurant or supermarket or retail shop's consumers to proplong their staying time to make consumption decisions. Hence, it seems that music facility environment can raise consumers' consumption desire in possible.

● University bookstore atmospheric factors how to influence student's purchase book behavior?

Any university bookstore how to do international control and structuring of book internal environment to raise students' purchase book desires in university itself school's bookstore, it will be one popular question to any universities. Hence, whether the university bookstore internal (FM) factors include: lighting, music, colors, scents, temperature, layout and general cleanliness as well as university external factors include: the university bookstore shape/size, windows, university parking facility for students availability and location,which can play an influential role of the university bookstore image in order to influence the university itself students to choose to buy books from themselves bookstore or university outside bookstores.

Whether the university student needs to spend how long individual learning time and how mcuh learning nervous to spend time to choose any kinds of book in the univeristy bookstore or outside bookstores, this issue , he/she will consider. Because he/she does want to expect spend much time and nervous to choose to buy books in any bookstore. If the universitt's bookstore physical location and internal (FM) desing image can let its target student customers to feel it's all book products are stored in any attractive internal book shelves places, e.g. the cheapest and the most expensive different subjects of text books are stored in one system method to bring the positive image of value snd quality in order to let university target student customers can find their books' choice location to spend less time to search any books to read in the unversity bookstore easily.

However, due to learning time is shortage to every university student of the universty's book shelves can display all text books in the attractive right locations in the university bookstore as well as the university's bookstore ought has an adequate space to let university students to walk to anywhere and find any subjects of text books and compare their book sale prices in the bookstore's any shelves' locations easily when they walk to the subject of book shelf location, then they can make accurate decision either to buy the right kind of subject book or not buy it to read in the short time. They will ferl their book choice purchase decision making process won't influence their learning time in themselves univeristy. Then, the university students will be influenced by themselve university's bookstore's attractive external university facilites in the univeristy's any teaching places and the university's bookstore internal attractive environment facility image which can influence the students to make final choices to buy their liking books to read from their university's itself bookstore. Hence, the university's bookstore internal and external building environment (FM) design factors will influence its students whether choose to buy from themselves bookstore or another outside general bookstore.

● How and why does retail atmospheric environment influence consumers behavior in retail shop?

Any shop's internal facility management design can influence atmospheric environment to influence consumer individual shopping desire, e.g. colour, lighting, music, crowding, design and layout factors, which internal shop (FM) environment can influence the first time shopping visiting client ' cognitive process how to feel the shop store image. Such as if the store's (FM) environment can bring enjoyable and fun and happy image to let them to feel shopping's enjoyment.

In conclusion, when consumers will like to stay longer time in the store. Due to the store's internal (FM) atmospheric environment can attract them to stay longer time in the store. Then, the customer's shopping value will raise and it can bring purchasing intention and shopping satisfaction. How can (FM) influence retail atmospheric physical (FM) environment ? Can (FM) bring indirect relationship to influence how the consumer individual causes positive or negative purchase intention when he/she has influence to proplong staying desire in the store, when the shop has good (FM) , it will bring long time to make consumption chance in the shop.

Facility management brings what benefits to entertainment theme parks

In entertainment theme park organizations, they must need to have different kinds of leisure playing machine facilities to supply to visitors to choose to play. So, facility management (FM) must need to imrpove any one entertainment theme parkj machine facility quality, it aims to avoid accidents occur , due to any leisure machine facilities are old or damage when they are used to operate in daily long opening time. Hence, FM must be needed to improve any entertainment theme parks' different kinds of leisure playing machine equipment frequently. If any one theme park leisure machine facility has poor FM in order to improve its machine quality. Consequently, this kind of leisure theme park leisure playing mahcine may be sudden to bring accidents occur, when any one visitor chooses this one of leisure playing machine facility to play. It may cause the player to hurt, even die in possible. Hence, FM to any entertainment theme park playing machine equipment , it may be one major facility repair management srtategy to any entertainment theme parks leisure playing machine facilities, because any one leisure playing machine facilities may bring any one visiot body hurt when the playing machine is old. Instead of FM can bring safety and playinf machine facilities quality improvement benefits to any one entertainment theme park leisure playing machine, whether FM to entertainment theme parks can bring psotive playing of leisure emotion to any one theme park visitor. I shall attempt to discuss as below:

Firstly, we need to know that any kinds of entertainment theme parks why they need to implement FM strategy. Why FM can bring advantages to any kinds of entertainment theme parks. In fact, the benefits of facility management to entertainment theme parks, it enables a more cost-effective working process within any kinds of the theme park any leisure playing machine facilities, such as theme park leisure playing sevice business. It improves the efficiency and it can help the theme park to manage health and safety requirements in accordance with industry regulations. It increases lifespan of a theme park any kinds of leisure playing machines, they are the theme park fixed assets, such as theme park's any kinds of leisure playing machine facilities. New theme parks and attractions can also improve the image of a destination increase tourism and hence economic benefits for the local community , and provide education and entertainment opportunities to the public.

Hence, it is common sense, if the theme park can have good FM to improve its any leisure playing facilities in order to avoid any accident occurrence , when any one visitor chooses to play its any one lesiure machine. Then, it can bring positive safe emotion feeling to satisfy any one visitor whose individual playing safe need to any kinds of playing leisure machines. I believe that its visitors number will not decrease, even increases significantly forever. Hence , the major roles of a theme park facility manager, is that to ensure the upkeep and manintenance of its any one entertainment playing machines, e.g. rolling rides, water rides etc. So, that they meet both safety and health standards to let any one visitors to feel safe to play.

In fact, the scope of facilities management covers two main areas: space and infrastructure , such as planning, design and workplace, construction, occupancy , maintenance and furniture as well as people and organization (such as catering, cleaning and HR, hospitality, accounting and marketing efficient operation in office) both aspects. Hence, these are 6 main facilities to ensure one available for any familiry theme plars. For leisure theme park case, rides and attractions are needed for all ages of any one theme park visitors. This is perhaps the most imprtant, as different parks will have different target audiences, e.g. refreshments, shops, toilets, and parking , access facilities and any one kind of leisure playing machines, such as rolling rides, water rides etc.

Hence, a theme park is a type of amusement park that bases its choice of which kinds of leisure playing facility structures and attractions around a central theme often featureing multiple areas with different themes. Unlike temporary and mobile fun fairs and carnivals, amusement parks are stationary and built for long lasting operation. Hence, every theme park must need have a photogenic, iconic landmark that draws people into the park, beautiful landscaping , enough available attraction capacity to keep peak waits for non-new attractions under 90 minutes, all of these are other faciliities. They must also need to manage to keep more attraction to theme park any one visitor to feel enjoyable and comfortable to play any one theme park leisure playing machines.

What advantages to the theme park implements FM strategy? For Ocean Park example, it aims to let visitors feel themed ocean animal recreational and educational and leisure park experience. So, it must need to upgrade to improve its any facilities to avoid long time repair spending expenditure. FM project may include: modifying sections of ocean park road, which is a local distributor, around the existing bus terminus , drain works, tunneling and geotechnical works, bulk excavation and slope works, site clearance, modification to bus terminus, taxi stands as well as utilities works including power supply distribution, electrical substations, freshwater and saltwater reservoirs, water supply distribution, gas supply distribution, telecommunications networks, landscope irrigation network to the ocean park any one ocean fish reservoirs, primary life support system works for animal keeping, area development works include elevated walkways, external lighting, external escalators, bridges, parkwide systems works include: signage, background, music system, toilet facilities, guard sheds, first and facilities, communication systems , CCTV systems and waste facilities, landscape or theming works, themed concern pavements, hardscape soft landscaping, water and rockwork features, visual intrusion screens, area props and artwork etc. works for the attractions venues include: animal exhibits, marine animal, terrestrial animal, aviaries , bind exhibits, individual life support systems for animal , exhibits and non-animal related attractions, e.g. shipwreck play area, bamboo maze etc. installation of rides interactive rides , transportation rides etc. , works for venues include : event halls, outdoor live show area, cinema band stands, work for the merchandise / retail facilities include souvonir stores, novelty stores, games ascade, photo shops etc. in the ocean park.

Moreover, any ocean park also have works for the food and baverage facilities include: restaurants, ballery, food casrts as well as back of house facilities include: ocean park offices, break areas, warehouses , centralized facilities, operational facilities etc. , even the ocean park inside hotel development facilities. All of these may bring positive or negative leisure activities impacts to influence any one of this ocean park visitor individual emotion significantly, if he /she feel comfortable and enjoyable , when they enter this ocean park. This ocean park whole natural environment may influence they like to stay long time in this ocean park. So, when they can stay long time in this ocean park, they may spend money to live hotels, spend money to play any leisure machines and spend time to go to shopping, or buying tickets to see any movies in this ocean park. All of this ocean park natural environment facilities and leisure playing machines improvement may influence any one visitor individual emotion either negative or positive feeling.

On conclusion, any theme parks must need to implement FM strategy to improve their theme parks inside natural environment and leisure playing machines quality and hotel living facilities and theme park external transport tool stations facilities, e.g. taxi, bus , railway station distance to convenience any one visitor can catch any one kind of public transport tool to arrive this theme park in short time easily. Also, any theme parks need to impove environment facilities in order to let any one visitor feels comfortable and enhoyable feeling when they choose this theme park to play. Consequently, the theme park's visitors number may be influenced to increase by their positive playing emotion feeling.

Facility management brings what advantages to theatres

Theatre performance needs performers own proficient performance skills to perform their music, or art performances to let audiences feel happy and satisfactory to see or listen their performances in the theatre hall, instead of performers their individual performing factor. Facility management (FM) in the theatre any facilities, e.g. performing hall, toilets, seats, theatre cater restaurants, car parking location etc. different theatre inside and outside facilities may also influence any one theatre audience whether he / she can feel enjoyable to see or listen any one art or music perfofmance, because if they feel the theatre facilities are poor quality. This theatre poor facilities feeling factor may also influence they expect to go to this theatre to see any art performances or listen any music performance again. Hence, instead of theatre performancers their individual performance skillful factor, any theatres their whole theatre inside and outside facilities will may also influence any one theatre music or art audience to choose to buy ticket to enter this theatre to see or listen any performances again. So, any one theatre facilities satisfactory feeling may also be another important factor to influence the theatre performance tickets sale number. I shall attempt to indicate the different kinds of facilities aspects, that any one theatre ought need to considerate their facilities improvement aspects issue as below:

Firstly, we need to know whether what theatre essential facilities elements may be. Then, I shall discuss how to manage theatre facilities in orde to improve its performance to assist any one performance to raise their performance level and bring more listening music or seeing art performance satisfactory and comfortable feeling to every theatre audience, when they are sitting one to two hours, even more than two hours in the theatre/

Hence, whole theatre inside facilities may influence any one audience individual satisfactory feeling, instead of seeing the art performers or listening the music performers their performances in the theatre halls. Although any one theatre audience makes decision to buy the ticket that their aims is general listening the music performance or seeing the art performance., but when they must need to sit long time in the theatre seats to enjoy any performances in the theatre, the extra (another) theatre facilities factor may also influence their satisfacgory feeling, e.g. if the theatre performance is music performance, all audience feel the theatre sound system facilities are poor to influence their listening music performance satisfactory feeling, e.g. more noise or feeling difficulty to listen soft music from the performers. Then, the whole music performance quality will be influenced to worse listening standard leve, it is not due to the music performer individual music playing skillful aspect, it is possible due to the theatre whole music sound system facilities or music sound equipment can not achieve the actural music sound satisfactory listening performance standard level effect to let any one music audience feels difficulty to listen the music performers how play their music performance proficiently.

So, it seems that theatre music sound system facilities may influence any one music performance standard level to be worse to the whole music poor performance process. It is not possible to any one music performance individual music playing skills whether he can play proficient music sound system facilities to improve or repair frequently to cause the whole music performance quality level to become worse indirectly. Hence, theatre music sound system facilities which may influence whole music performance level either to raise or reduce indiirectly.

Any theatre needs to be created the facility and workflow management module to coordinate events, perople and resources across organization;s available venues in order to pull down from and create information in the theatre database to manage theatre venue, staff and audiences. Because covid 19 disease occurs, it influences many theatres need to keep clean seating environment to avoid any one owning covid 19 disease audience enters the theatre easily. So, the theatre cleaning seating managing method and crowd controlling quese method both aim to avoid covid 19 disease occurrence in the theatre,. when any one theatre staff or audience enter the theatre. So, any theatre cleaning and safe FM must be raise improvement level.

The theatre FM seating managing needs to conside: The occuring in different venues, the theatre resources needed at each location at a particular time, theatre staff memebers needed at diffeent locations or times, e.g. which events are occurring in each venue, the theatre resources needed at each location at a location, tasks requiring completion from quick 1- perspon to do items to entire operations involving several people like set construction or rehearsal before any performances began in the theatre, an ordering of tasks and dependence on each other , ie parinting can not begin until construction is completed and grouping of similar items together.

Hence, when the theatre can orgainze one effective FM strategy , it may help the theatre organization and art/music performance organization to arrange those tasks efficiently, such as scheduling: people (theatre staffs, performaners, theatre places, e.g. venues , theatre resources / supplies , e.g. every art/ music performance project), distribution (calendars can be updated internally before whole month all theatres performances begin in order to any performance time can be viewed on the theatre internet), billing (creating a quote and administration tasks). So, theatre daily taskj list, meeting scheduling, with staffs email notification etc. theatre administration tasks can be influenced to raise efficience when the theatre can have effective FM strategy.

In general, theatre is one music / art performance venue (place). It may include: theatre venue, space management, building maintenance, testing and inspection management , such as covid 19 disease is for every theatre audience before they can permit to enter the theatre as well as theatre staffs, performers and audience body contact management in the theatre hall inside any environment that they can stay long time in the clean theatre environment. SO, effective anf efficient organized to any one performance, theatre FM ought need to keep any one whole performance process in safe and clean working environment, e.g. theatre task facilities are safe, and theatre audiences and theatre staffs and performers , they can contact in safe and clean crowd theatre environment often.

In fact, Fm in theatre , it uses specialized theatre knowledge to provide technical direction and control over all theatre systems, including sound, lighting, projections, riugging, counterweight system, and front of house procedures involved with productions with an emphasis on safety. Hence, FM in theatrical environment is the definition of four core values. They may include: responsibility means to guarantee all the theatre installations to be in perfect condition and work properly every simgle day; flexibility means to work day and nught to finish maintenance work before the theatre audiences arrive for another daily performance, passion means to deliver the best theatre experience for the theatre audiences controlling all elements in services, ambitions means besides showing the best musical shows on stage in one of the beautiful theatres. So, FM intheatre may include: security, climate contol, cleaning, mechancial, music sound system management, engineering, electronics, reception system management, mail, fire protection, lighting, maintenance, rehearsal performance facility arrangement etc. for the theatre performance before and after service in order to achieve the saisfactory performance to let auiences to feel.

On conclusion, any nowadays theatre organizations must need have effective and efficient facility management (FM) stategy in order to let audiences to feel safe and confident and comfortable feeling when they are sitting down in the seats to spend long time to listen or see any kinds of art or music performances in the theatre hall. So, when they feel the theatre can provide comfortable and safe and clean inside theater hall environment to see or listen any art or music performances. Consequently, the theatre ticket sale number may be influenced to raise in possible. So, I can explain why any theatres ought need FM to assist themselves theatre operation

facility management second main function

Facility management improving efficiency and service quality function

Why do many organizations begin to feel facility management importance? What are the real functions that when one organization can attempt to achieve facility management strategy? The main functions of facility managment may include. For example, when sale manager is is directly responsible for managing the performance of salespeople, facility managment seems that it can not help any salepsople to increase sale number, they have no direct relatonship, but in fact, any salespeople must need to stay to sell any products in the shop. SO, the shop's facility environment may have indirect relationship to influence customers purchase emotion, when they enter the shop. If the shop's facility is more attractive, it may let customers to feel comfortable to stay long time in the shop.

So, facility management influences people, processes, the building and technology to be improveed better in order to achieve good job performance or sale performance both in possible. This serves many broader goals, improving efficiency, and productivity and creating a positive workplace culture, coordinating desking arrangements, managing employees, facilitating moves and spaces utilization, handling emergency planning benefits to any organizations.

Hence, the facility management function to service aspect, they may include submitting a work order request rapidly (raising efficiency) , when the shop can be designed to have more space for service staffs to contact customers , it aims to let they feel comfortable to stay in the shop, reserving space and visitors and handling emergency action planning more easily. When the shop customer service counters have have effective enquiry place facility enviroment for customers and customer service staffs in order to let they can feel comfortable to stay to enquire and answer in the shop's service counters in long time.

ON physical building improvement aspect, effective facility management many provide repair, maintenance, and building improvement, workplace , cleaning , on-and-off site property management , e.g. improving security places to avoid theft occurrence easily. Moreover, more importance is needed for facility managers to understand and use technology, workplace management system aggregate data, which drives crucial decisions about how to run the business and shape the workplace, a modern facility management building, offices , factories , shops even living houses in order to raise amart building concept comfortable feeling to let house owners, shops staffs and customers factories workers, office staffs to feel smart facility management system lay let them to feel comfortable when they are working or living in the smart building. So, amart facility management system may bring these functions: Researching IOT devices based on data collection needs, integrating IOT devies into everyday facilities processes, determining the cost, ROI and using aggregated data to better understand the workplace.

Hence, in one smart building, facility management system can collect and analyze data from networked technologies to get insights about the workplace. This fuels better decision-making on how to optimize the work environment for the people using it. For example, all smart office technology relies on data collection , access control system supports safety, when automation technological streamlines processes. And when these's a data component to any networked device or software, the true benefit of most technology is in its function. So, future smart offices , houses, factories etc. building will be needed to apply facility management technology to let any one feels comfortable when they need to use the building smart office or house or factory automatic turn off light facility when the office facility management system can help all the building all offices to turn off the light or central air condition automatically in order to save power or reduce energy waste in any office inside working environment any time when the facility management samart system ensure that none any one is staying in the building any offices.

Hence, facility management ought bring these benefits to any business office users or house living users, they may include tha complete management and maintenance of the buildings, people and assets of the business, it enables a more cost-effective working process within the business, it improves the efficiency of the business, e.g. raising workers productivities when they need to stay long time in the factory to manufacture any products, if they feel the factory environment is more comfortable and safe to let them to work, their emotion may be influenced to feel more happy to work, even raising the product manufacturing number more efficienly, it improves the efficiency of the business, it helps to manage health and safety requirements in accordance with industry requirement, helping a workplace run at maximum efficiency, e.g. cost reduces, space optimization , creating a comfortable feeling in a better workplace, outsourcing facility management service may brings better service delivery, more variety snf flexibility, today's employees and tenants expect more then just clean restrooms and adquate lighting to create and enhance great company cultures.

So, FM provides and manages a variety , it supports services in order to organize all the organization's functions more efficiently. It focuses on the integration of primary activities on both strategic and operational levels. Moreover, facilities management can be defined as the tools and services that support the functionality, safety and sustainability. For outsourcing facilty managmeent advantage., it may involve turning over the complete management and decision making authority of an operation to somebody outside organization. It may help businesses to maximize returns on investment and establish long term competitive advantage in the markplace. Hence, the types of facility management may include: cleaning, hardware inspection and maintenance, transportation, security service, fire safety. However, there are some differences between facilities management function and property management funciton. In general, facility management and office management are concerned with the people using the space, when property management concerned with the space itself only, e.g. the physical building shell and rented offices etc. buildings.

Facility management brings what benefits
Facility managmnt brings what benefits to organization
Can facility management bring social benefits? What benefits do facility management bring to our societies? What are social responsibilities to facility management? Why do our societies need facility managment services? I shall attempt to explain as below:
IN fact, ay organizations will need facilities management services, because it can bring continuous development benefits on economy, environment and society aspects, e.g. minimising waste to landfill form the organization, when the organization has effective facility managment service, increasing supply chain opportunities, when the organization can apply facility management skill to arrange how to let worehouse or store space can keep goods to put on corrective positions and more space to put their goods

in warehouse. So goods can be transported to move more easily when the warehouse can have effective transportation to different countries more efficiently in short delivering time as well as when global warewhouses can have effective facility management service to be arranged how to store their goods in warehouses efficiently in order to bring rapid transportation benefits between the country and another country. It is significant " rapid goods transportation deliving benefit" to any organizations. For Amazon example, it needs to manage different goods to keep to its different countries warehouses in order to transport goods to fly to different countries customers‘ homes every day by air plane rapidly every day. If Amazon can have effective warehouse facility management strategy to manage how its different kinds of goods to be putted on its shelves in its different countries warehouses. Then, it's logistic workers won't need spedn much time to seek any goods on shelves in order to deliver their goods to fly to another country in short time efficienly. So, Amazon warehouses facilties managment service can help its organization to provide efficient delivering service.

How can facility managers satisfy the needs of customer when such needs changing so frequently to their organizations? Organizational justify theory indicates that where managers do not have resources available tomeet employee demands. The procedures used to divide what resources are available may be used to achieve satisfaction. How can facility management satisfy needs of customers when both these needs and environments in which they are operating change as frequently? How to match unpredictable space demand with supply? How to manage refurishment of out dated facilities, dealing with the competing space and service demand of different deparrments.

So, it brings this question: How can facility and accommodation management groups appease their customers in the intermediate term? SO, it seems that facility management can raise our social organizational justice benefits, such as improving service performance and raising customer satisfactory feeling for the organization's efficient service performance.

IN fact, efficient facility management strategy may help our social any organizations to earn these benefits. They may include: Influencing empllyees' perceptions fair procedural fairness in our social orgnaizations, the provision of timely feedback and effecgtive communication of the basis for decisions. So, effective facility management may help global organizational managers to know hoe to allocate new space that has become available to let employees to feel enjoyment to work in order to raise efficiencies or improve productivities. It will create any country's GDP growth when the organization can implement effective facility management strategy. Hence facility management can bring benefits to improving customer satisfactions, improving productivities and raising efficiencies. Then, our social organizations will have more social benefits, when GDP growht is caused by facility management service improvement to any global organizations.

Brochner (2003) pints out the reality that innovation in jointly FM brings benefits to organizations , developing goods and associated services in manufacturing is starting to surface, when the connection between facillity design and management is still weak, IN organizations, FM can meet organizational business need more appropriately, atract customers more are easier to manage and controp and operated more cost effectively, respond better to occupant needs.

After all, design has an effect on sales efficiency, staff, profit , capital investment, and maintenance cost(Ransley and lngram , 2001). These factors are the concern of facility management as much as they relate to the organization's core business success. Therefore, managing FM requirements during design is necessary for an organization to achieve its goals after occupancy a newly build facility.

For airport facility management case example, an effective management of the facility , aimed at successfully satisfying both the airport ownership and the passegners (air plane travellers) customers, should be based on agreement, network and strategic allience with FM functoins from other airports, they can apply outsourcing FM strategy to provide facility management service during travellers are staying in their airports, they can feel enjoyment in airport environment, then their shopping desire and again visiting the country's airport desire will be influenced to raise, when the country's airport can provide comfortable FM airport facility to let them to feel. Hence, FM can raise customer service perofrmance with firm's objective and service processes, drive performance improvement and increase client satisfaction, such as airport travelling places whehter how FM may influence travellers to stay how long time in the country's airport. It means that when the airport is more attraction, e.g. design is attration. Then , the airport can persuaded travellers to stay long time in the airport. Consequently, their shopping chance will increase in the airport.

Facility managment brings what benefits to economy
The economic benefits of FM organizational design . Evidence is growing that FM may help buildings provide financial rewards for building owners, operators and occupants. FM buildings typically have lower annual costs for energy, water, maintenance / repair, reconfiguring space because of changing needs, and other operating expenses. These reduced costs do not have to some at the expense of higher first costs, Through FM design and innovative use of high quality of materials and equipment, the first cost of FM building can be the same as or lower than that of a traditional building. Morevoer, some sustainable design features have higher first cost, but the payback period for the incremental investment often is short and the lifecycle cost typically lower than the cost of more traditional buildings. In additional to direct cost savings, FM buildings can provide owener and socieyt benefits, for example, FM building features can promote better health, comfort, well being and productivity of buildings, occupants , which can reduce levels of absenteeism and increase productivities. Moreover, FM buildings can also often owners economic benefits form lower risks, longer building lifetimes, improveed ability to attract new employees, when they feel office environment or warehouse , shop working environment are more comfortable to let they feel, when they are staying in these FM workplaces, reduced expenses for dealing with complaints, and increasing asset value.
Overall, Fm buildings also offer society as a whole economic benefits, such as reduced cost fomr air pollution , damage, avoiding landfills, wastewater treatment plant, power plants and distribution lies. So, low first cost and later repair / manintenance expense reducing or avoiding. Consequently, above of these will be FM building's long time economnic benefits, social benefits and organizational benefits to the building owner, its clients and our societies.

Facility management can reduce
maintenance service expenditure
Facility management provides a variety of non core operations and maintenance services to support any organizations' operation. For logistic organization example, it is possible to provide effective maintenance service to warehouse in order to reduce warehouse facilities to be damaged to bring to spend to buy any new equipment facilities expenditure. So, when the logistic compnay's warehouse facilities can be maintenanced to be the best quality. Then, they can be used these warehouses' machines facilities again.

Their performance can assist workers to manufacture any products to keep the most efficiently an raising the best production performance in whole manufacturing process. Then, this logistic company's facility management department can bring to avoid purchase any new machine facilities expenditure spending. One to these warehouses' production machine facilities are kept in the best productin performance environment evem in long term production need.

The logistic industry's facility management department can create cost savings and efficiency of the warehouse's workplaces. It's machines facilities (producton machines) are dealt with the maintenance management of the physical assets maintenance service. FM (facilities management) has been being applied to industrial facilities in logistic and warehouse industry long term as well as maintenance plays a significant role to ensure the full service and the warehousing system, including both building components and equipment in warehouse.

Maintenance service is needed to bring a certain level of availability and reliability of a warehouse facilities system and its components and its ability perform to a standard level of quality. So , it seems that logistic industry's warehouse asset cost reducing. It depends on whether it has one facility management deparrment to provide maintenance service to itself warehouse workplace's production machine facilities and warehouse building itself in order to let workers t feel the manufacturing machines can bring good manufacturing performance to assist them to produce any products in one safe warehouse workplace environment. Hence, the performance measurement of warehouse maintenance issue will be valued to be consider to every warehouse manager and facility manager in logistic industry.

In logistic industry, (FM) works at two level on the one hand, it provides a safe and efficient working environment, which is essential to influence warehouse workers whether how they perform to do their manufacturing tasks or logistic goods delivery tasks in warehouse. When they feel the warehouse is safe environment to work. They will not need to consider anywhere has risk to cause they die by accident in warehouse. Hence, they can concentrate on doing their every tasks . On the other hand, it can involve strategic issues, such as property (warehouse workplace and management, strategy property decision and warehouse facility, e.g. manufacturing macine, facility maintenance and checking planning and maintenance planning development.

However, reducing the operating expense issue will be the main aim when the logistic company feels that it has need to set up one in-house facility management department to carry on any maintenance service for its warehouses' any workplace property and manufacturing machines facilities. So, when the logistic company decides to implement one facility management department, it needs to ensure its facility management department can bring the minimum level of keeping manufacturing performance and efficiency to its warehouses' any manufacturing machines and warehouses' property to avoid to be damaged in shourt term, such as loss of busness due to failure in service, provision of project to customer satisfaction, provision of safe environment, effective utilisation of workplace space, e.g. warehouse effectiveness and communication between the workers and the logistic managers in the warehouse workplace , due to the warehouse's space is not enough maintenance service reliability to the logistic company's warehouse, responsiveness of the warehouse's worker individual negative emotion problem, due to hs/she often feels need to work in one unsafe warehouse working environment. Hence, it seems that poor or unsafe warehouse working environment can influence workers feel negative emotion to work to bring low efficiency (inefficiency) or under productive performance in warehouse. It has relationship to influence they to bring psychological negative emotion feeling to work when the organization lacks one effective warehouse management repairing service to be provided to the warehouse's facilities and properties' maintenance needs in order to avoid ineffective measurement and misleading of performance.

Hence, the logistic company's facilities management department often needs to be reviewed whether irs maintenance service level is passed to achieve the lowest repair (maintenance) service standard to its warehouse itseld property and manufacturing machine or warehouse delivery tool facilities or warehouse lamps' light whether is enourh to let workers to see anything clearly to avoid accident occurrence or see anything to work clearly or the warehouse space areas are enough to let they can have enough space to walk or communicate to their team supervisors or deliver any goods more easily in the short distance between the worker's sending goods location and the delivering goods destination in order to avoid because the lacking enough space to cause the accident occurrence , due to the space is not enough to let they deliver their goods to any locations in warehouse.

Hence, it seems logistic company's (FM) department can contribute to the organization's mission, such as avoiding warehouse accident occurrence, inefficiency, inadequancy and unavailability of the facility for future needs when the warehouse lacks enough space areas to bring poor performance of facility and dangerous warehouse itself property in warehouse, e.g. safe and reliable operations of material handling equipment and maintenance of warehouse facilities, grounds, sesurity system, utilities, plumbing, heating , enough lightins system, air conditioning, warming heater, fire protecton, security system alarm etc. facilities in warehouse.

Hence, it seems that if the logistic company expected to reduce to spend lot of excessive manufacturing machine purchase expenditure, lossing of workers' life or bring workplace accidents , due to poor warehouse workplace environment, even bringing lawsuit compensation claim loss , due to the worker individual accident or death is caused from the poor warehouse facilities, or bring negative emotion to let the workers feel they are working in unsafe warehouse workplace environment. Then, it ought choose to set up on facility manageemtn department in order to provide enough maintenance service to its warehouse to avoid these non essential expenditure causing , due to these poor warehouse facilities factors.

Hence any logistic company ought choose to set up one itself in -house facility management department, it be better than outsourcing its all facilities service to one facility mangement (maintenance service provider) to help it to deal any kinds of maintenance service in warehouse. Because it is long term maintenace need to its warehouse's any machines and warehouse itself properties. If it chose to find one outsourcing facilitiy management maintenance service provider to replace its in-house facility mangement department to deal all related facilities maintenance tasks in warehouse. Then, it is possible that it needs to pay long time facilities maintenance service fee to its outsourcing facility management maintenance service provider more than itself facility management maintenance service provision department.

In conclusion, to decide whether the company ought need or not need facilities maintenance service or either set up in-house facility management department or outsource one facility management maintenance service provider. It depends on whether its organization has how many facilities are used in its workplace, how many staffs are working the workplace, how much size of its workplace, its workplace is office or warehouse or factory, how long time of its facilities' useful time etc. factors , then it can decide whether it needs or does not need one facility maintenance service deparment or outsouring facility maintenance service provider to help it to deal any facilities management problem in its organization.

Facility management role in
organization

When one company feels that it has need facility management service. It can choose to set up either in-house facility management department or seek one outsourcing facility management service provider to help it to arrange any facility management service need. However, this facility management role is only one for the organization. It concerns this question: What facility management maintenance function can bring the benfits to the organization?

It can define that all services required for the management of building and real estate to maintain and increase their value, the means of providing maintenance support, project management and user management during the building life cycle, the integration of multi-disciplinary activities within the built environment and the mangement of their impact upon people and the workplace. In traditional, (FM) services may include building fabric maintenance, decoratin and refurbishment, plant, plumbing and drainage maintenance, air conditioning maintenance, lift and escalator maintenance , fire safety alarm and fire fighting system maintenance, minor project management. All these are hard services. Otherwise, cleaning , security, handyman services, waste disposal, recycling, pes control, grounds maintenance, internal plants. All tese are soft services. Additional services, might also include: pace planning, things moving management, business risk assessment, business continuity planning, benchmarking, space management, facilities contract outsourcing service arrangement, information systems, telephony, travel booking facility utility management, meeting room arrangement services, catering services, vehicle fleet management, printing service, postal services, archiving , concierge services, reception services, health and safety advice, environmental management.

All of these services will be every organiztion's in-house facility soft or hard services needs. So, it explains why some large organizations feel need one effective facility management department to help them to arrange how to implement facility serivices efficiently in order to achieve cost reducing, raising efficiency and performance improvemen aims because one effective facility management control system can influence employee individual productive effort to be raised or reduced indirectly.

However, (FM) can be selected either setting up one in-house (FM) department or outsourcing its services to one facility mangement service provider to help the organizatin to solve any kinds of facilities maintance service problems. One on-house (FM) department is a team, it needs employees to deliver all (FM) services. Some specialist services are needed to be outsourced, when the service is on expertise in the company. The no expertise services will be outsourced to simple service contracts, e.g. lift and escalator (FM) department will have direct labour, but it can outsource some specialist to help it to do some complect facilities management service. So, the team leader can of can manage whose team staffs, such as maintenance technicians run low risk operations . Otherwise, the outsourcing facility management service provider needs to help it to operate high risk operations or maintenance vital plant facility management service. Anyway, it can set up in-house (FM) department to arrange specialist direct labour and outsourced (FM) services to more than one facility management service providers to do different kinds of (FM) services. One of these outsourcing (FM) service provider, who can arrange sub-contractors to assist it to finish any (FM) services of it's outsourcing (FM) services are more complex to compare the other sub-contractors (third parties).

● What is a facility manager's role to provide quality service to satisfy its user needs?

We need to know how quality can be defined in facility management and why it should be defined by the customer? How facility managers can find out customer (user) needs? What are the difficulties in finding out users' needs and in delivering quality services? Whether improving quality always means requiring higher cost?

In general, facility manager's major responsibilities may include these major functional areas: longer range and annual facility planning, facility financial forecasting, real estate acquisiton and/or disposal, work specification, installation and space management, architectural and engineering planning and design, new construction and/or renovation, maintenance and operations management, maintenance and operation management, telecommunications integration, security and general administrative services. When the facility manager had implemented any one of these FM services for those user. How does he/she provide excellent (FM) service quality ot let whose users to feel satisfactory?

In fact, quality issues can not be considered without customer-oriented perspective service quality involves a comparision of expectation with performance. (FM) service quality is a measure of how well to service level delivered matches customer expectation. So, these issues are (FM) service user's general measurement level requirement. The (FM) manager needs to achieve these the minimum performance measurement level to satisfy whose (FM) user's needs.

However, (FM) service quality has three characteristics: Intangibility, heterogeneity, inseparability. But in fact, (FM) service delivered may be through tangible physical aspects, e.g. factory plant workplace building, machine equipment maintenance, intangible (FM) services, e.g. managing space moving in plant to let staffs to work, managing outsourcing cleaners to clean factory equipment. However, all (FM) service performance often varies, due to the behavior of service personnel. Hence, a well developed job specification and training can help to improve the consistence of services of (FM). Any (FM) productin and consumption of many services may are inseparable and they are ususally interactions between the (FM) client and the contact person from the service provider.

Hence, it seems that service quality is considered as hard to evaluate. In (FM) service quality, it includes physical quality and interactive non-physical service quality. Physical quality is tangibles: The appearance of the physical facilities, equipment, personnel and communication materials. Non-physical services quality means reliability: The ability to perform the promised service dependably and accurately; responsiveness means the willingness to help customers and provide promopt service to let user to feel; assurance mans the competence of the system in its credibility in providing a courteous and secure service and empathy means the approachability, ease of access and effort taken to understand customers' needs.

Hence, a good performance of (FM) manager , he/she ought satisfy the user's tangible and non-tangible both service quality needs. I recommend that he/she can attempt to predict what are the (FM) customer expects in each (FM) service needs. Then, it can make decision what aspect(s) will be the (FM) users major (FM) service need and what aspect(S) won't be the (FM) users major (FM) service need. Then, he/she can make more accurate decision to arrange time, human resource , cost spending amount arrangement whether when it ought concentrate on finishing the (FM) major service tasks as well as whether how he/she ought finish the major (FM) service tasks to be more easily, e.g. how to arrange staffs number to finish, how many the minimum staffs number is needed to be arrange the major (FM) service tasks, time arrangement is important factor, because it can influence whether he/she ought finish the major (FM) service tasks today or tomorrow or later in order to have enough time to finish other non-major (FM) service tasks. Instead of time management, staff number arrangement is also important factor , if he/she arrangeed the excessive staffs number to do the (FM) major services tasks, then it is possible that it will have shortage of staffs number to finish the non-major (FM) service tasks on the day. So, avoiding either majoe or non-major (FM) services can not finish on the day. The (FM) manager needs to predict when the major (FM) services and the non-major (FM) services which are necessary to be finished in order to have enough time and staffs to assist him/her to finish every day major and non-major (FM) servie effectively. Then, the achievement of his/her (FM) major and non-major tangible and non-tangible services , it will have more chance to be performed efficiently by his/her managed staffs.

In conclusion, in any organizations , (FM) manager needs have good predictable effort to evaluate whether when his/her managed team need to finish the major and/or non-major (FM) tasks as well as whether how he/she ought arrange the accurate time and staff number to finish any major and/or non-major (FM) service tasks on the day. Then, his/her leading of (FM) service team can be managed to work more efficiently in order to satisfy her/his (FM) service user's needs.

How (FM) space moving management
can bring valued add to organizations

There are interesting questions: How (FM) can bring value-add to avoid loss or earn more profit to the organization? Can it influence employees to raise performance and improve efficiency ? Some organizations' (FM) service need which is necessary in order to let employees can raise productivity.

It is based on these assumptions: I assume the organizations have completely either outsourced or in-house their (FM) facility management departments will gain more effect on added value than they have no (FM) function as well as organizations have a strong coordination with the (FM) department will gain more added value than organizations with a weak coordination. Organizations in the profit aim can gain more added value than organizations in the not for profit aim sectors.

In fact, any organization is difficult to confirm it has relationship between improving performance, raising efficiency and owning (FM) function in its organization. (FM) could have to do with the attraction of easy but incomplete indicators of efficiency rather than the necessarily and less direct measures if the effectiveness and the relevance of space moving useful management, e.g. whether building has the enough space to let employees to move to work easy in order to raise efficiency, whether the building has excessive furniture and equipment number and they are putted on wrong places to be caused employees move difficulty in the building in order to influence productive performance.

However, how to arrange space moving management to equipment, e.g. copying machines, faxes, productive machines, they are putted on the locations where have enough space to let employees to move to another locations. For example, the building floor has more than 50 employees, but its space is not enough to let these 50 employees to move to any locations to let them to feel easily often. Then, it is posible to cause they feel nervous pressure and they can feel difficult to work , when they are working in a small office space or factory space or warehouse space. Then, the consequence will be under-predictive efficiency or poor performance to any one of these 50 employees in this office or factory or warehouse.

" Facility management is responsible for coordinating all efforts related to planning, designing, and managing buildings and their systems, equipment, and furniture to enhance. The organizations abilty to compete successfully in a rapidly changing world." (F.Becker)

The author explains equipment, workplace internal space designing, furniture space putting location arrangement will have possible to influence employee individual productive performance or efficiency to be raised or reduced in the workplace. Hence, it seems that, in the value chain (FM) belongs to the activity part of the firm. To make the facilities cooperation with each office or factory or warehouse using space moving facility management. Facility space moving management must be linked strategically, tactically and operationally to other support activity to add value to the organization's office or factory or warehouse space moving management arrangement more effectively.

Thus, how to arrangement space moving management issue it will have possible to influence the organization's employee individual productive performance and efficiency in whose workplace. It seems that (FM) space moving management arrangement have indirect relationship to influence the organization's employee individual performance and efficiency , due to they need often to work in the workplace, if they feel moving difficulty , or excessive equipment , furniture number is putting into the small office, factory or warehouse locations, or they feel the office or factory or warehouse has excessive (a lot of) staffs number to work in the small space of office or factory or warehouse. Then, they can not concentrate nervous on finishing every tasks in possible. In long term, their efficiencies will be poor or inefficiencies or their performance won't be improved or causing poort performance in possible.

Instead of the not enough space moving and excessive staffs number factor, it will bring another question: Can enough information systems equipment cause a more efficient and improved performance to the organization staffs in the workplace?

I assume that the office has 100 employees and it has only ten copying machines. So it means that ten employees use one copying machine. Hence, it brings this question: Is it enough to provide only ten copying machines to average ten employees to use? It depends on other factors, e.g. whether any one of these 100 employees needs to print how many documents per day , whether the five copying machines' locations are far away to separate different locations or they are stored in one printing room in the office, whether the day has how many staffs are absent, whether the day has how many printing machine(s) is/ are broken to need to be repaired. Hence, these unpredictable external environment factors will influence whether the five copying machines number is enough to let these 100 employees to use in the office every day. Hence, facility manager ought need to spend to observe average their copying behaviors every day in order to make data record. Many employees need to use copy machines to print documents, average how many document's page number, they need to print, how much average time spending to print their documents, average how many staff absent number on the day. Even, if the all five copying machines are stored in the printing room, calculating the staffs number whether how many staffs need more than five minutes to walk to the printing room to print their documents many staffs need to spend five minute to walk to the printing room, and they have other urgent tasks to wait to finish. It is possible to influence their efficiency, due to they often need to spend more than five minutes to walk to the printing room to print documents. If there are many staffs need to often to print documents, but their printing task will have many time, e.g. 20 separate printing tasks. Then, they need to spend at least (20x5) 100 minutes to spend time to walk to the printing room to print their documents. It must influence that they should not finish the other urgent tasks on the day. If there are many staffs to spend much time to walk to the printing room in the least 20 separate printing time or more on that day. All the facility manager needs to evaluate whether all the five copy machines are stored in the printing room whether it is the best location decision or they ought need be separated to put on different office locations in their workplaces, even he/she ought need to evaluate whether it is enough copying machines number, when the office has only 5 copying machines. He/she ought need to buy more copying machines number to satisfy any one of these 100 employee individual copyiing task need.

In conclusion, effective office or factory or warehouse space moving facility management will be one part task of (FM) function. If the office or factory or warehouse can have accurate equipment, machine , furniture number to avoid excessive or shortage number problem to cause employees often feel moving difficult problem in their workplace when they need to move to another location to work in office or warehouse or factory as well as whether the staff needs often spend time to wait the another employee to use the copying machine to print whose document or fax machine to deliver whose document. Then, it is not that fax or printing machines number is not enough to provide the employees to use in the office or warehouse or factory workplace.

Hence, (FM) includes space moving facility management to equipment , machines, furniture number as well as choosing anywhere is(are) the suitable location (s) arrangement to putting or storing these facilities in workplace as well as decision of the staff number and the workplace area size whether it has excessive staffs number to cause these staffs need to work in the small area size of office or warehouse or factory workplace. So, the organization ought need to decide whether it needs to reduce the office's staffs number to let them to work in another more suitable locations in another workplace. Hence, all these facilities space moving management and staffs and workplace size issues will be (FM) manager's consideration issues, because these external environment factors will influence employee individual efficiency and performance to be ppor to cause low valued to its organization in long term in possible .

Reference

Becker, F. (1990). " Facility management : a cutting edge field?" property management 8 (2): 25-28.

CHAPTER V

MTR (UNDERGROUND TRAIN) TRANSPORTATION SERVICE MARKET FACILITY MANAGEMENT

Predictive the choosing right
data asset and (FM) analytics
solutions to boost public
transportation service quality

Can gather the choosing right data public transportation service station facilities asset and analytics, it can give recommendation to help any organizatin to boost service quality? (FM) analytics data can be applied to public transportation service industry to be supported how and why the train, train, ferry , ship, air plane, underground train public transportation tools' time arrival and leaving information notice board and automated ticket paying machines facilities are putting on or stored any where locations in order to boost passengers to feel their facilities locations are convenient to let them to buy tickets and see the arrival and leaving time for the next public transportation tool from the information notice electronic board machine. So, it seems that these public transportation tools' station facilities locations can influence passengers to feel the public transportation service company how to consider to its passenger's buying ticket needs and next public transporation tool's arrival and leaving time information needs in order to boost its passenges use service quality and let them to feel better service reliable performance in any train, tram, ferry , ship, underground tram, airplane stations.

As these public transportation service organizations need to learn data analytics represent an opportunity for its ticket paying machine equipment facilities as well as the next transportation tool arrival and leaving time information notice board electronic equipment facilities anywhere the locations are the most suitable to put on or store these equipment to let passengers to walk to the ticket paying machines to buy the ticket to catch the train, tram, underground train, ferry, airplane, taxt, ship more easily. So, they do not need to spend more time to find these facilities locations and spend more time to queue to wait to buy ticket to catch the public transportation tool in stations conveniently. Instead of where is the seeking ticket paying machine location, where is the next public transportation tool arrival and leaving information notice time , these both issues will be any public transportion tool's passenger's main needs.

Hence, how to spend time to seek where the next public transportation tool's arrival and leaving time information electronic notice machine location and where the ticket paying machine location , these both factors will influence any passengers' positive or negative emotion causing. For example, if the passenger feels diffcult to find the ticket paying machine in the large area size train station or /and he/she feels difficult to find the train time arrival and leaving information to let him/her to know when the next train will arrive the station. Due to he/she feels difficult to find the train ticket paying machine, he/she needs to spend much time to find any one tickeet paying machine in the train station. Then, it will influence him/her to choose another public transportation tool to replace the train public transportation tool, e.g. he/she can choose to catch tram, underground train, taxi, bus, ferry, taxi, ship to replace train. So, it seems ticket paying machine and time arrival and leaving information notice electronic equipment 's location putting or stored choice will be one factor to influence the passenger to choose another kind of public transportation tool to replace train at the moment. When, he/she feels that he/she arrives the destination in the most short time. Then, the public transportation service organization (FM) manager has responsibility to evaluate whether there are enough ticket paying machines number to let passengers do not need to spend more time to queue to buy tickets to catch the public transporation tool in short time as well as there are enough time arrival and leaving for next transportation tool to let passengers to know. It will be their concerning issues when they arrive the public transportation service tool's station.

Hence, predictive passenger individual walking behavior can help the public transportation service organization to choose whether where are the most convenient and attractive locations to let the ticket paying machines and the arrival and leaving time information electronic board machines to be putted on or stored in the suitable station positions in order to let many passengers can find these essential facilities in stations very easily. So, gathering data concerns passenger walking behavior in the public transporation service any stations, which can help the facility manager to make more accurate evaluation to attempt to predict whether where the locations are common places to let passengers to choose to walk daily or where the locations are not common places to let passenger to choose not to walk daily in general. Then, he/she can apply these data of different locations in the stations to evaluate whether anywhere they will have many passengers to choose to walk or whether anywhere they won't have many passengers to choose to walk in order to make more accurate decision whether anywhere are the most suitable locations to let the ticket paying machines and the time arrival and leaving information electronic board equipment to be putter on or stored in order to let them to feel it is so easier to let them to find.

Anyway, calculating each station's passenger number per day issue is important to predict whether where , there are many passengers choose to walk or where, there are not many passengers choose to walk in these different public transportation service stations in order to evaluate whether where the stations' different ought put on paying ticket machines or time arrival and leaving information electronic boards in order to let they feel very easy to buy tickets and seeing the next arrival and leaving time information for the kind of public transportation service tool conveniently in the different stations. Moreover, if the station has no enough ticket paying machines number to be supplied to let passengers need to spend more than ten minute time to wait to buy ticket to catch the kind of public transportation service tool in every queue every day. Then it will cause them to choose another kind of public transportation tool to catch go to working place or entertainment place to replace it to on that day. Then, it will cause these passengers who often do not like to queue in the kind of public transportation service tool's any stations, who will not choose to go to anywhere of this kind of public transportation service tool's any stations again. Hence, in long term this kind of public tranportation service tool will lose many passengers. Thus, calculating each station's busy time of passengers number , which can predict when it is the busy time and it can make more accurate decision whether the station has need to increase enough ticket paying machines number in order to bring enough supply number to satisfy passengers' ticket purchase need in the busy time.

In conclusion, gathering above all stations' public transportation service equipment facilities number, storing positions datas and every station's passenger walking behavior datas, they are necessary to any public transportation tool service industry, because these equipments' number and storing locations will influence them to make decisions to choose another kind of public transportation tool to replace it's transportation service if they often feel difficult to find these facilities in its different stations. Thus, it is part of task to facility manager's responsibility if the public transportation service organization expects it won't lose many passengers , due to these external environment factor influence and it also implies cheap ticket price does not guarantee the passengers will choose to catch this kind of public tranportation service tool to go to anywhere.

The relationship between facility
management and productive
efficiency

It is one interesting question: Can facility management function bring benefits to raise productive efficiency to organizations? I shall indicate some cases to attempt to explain this possible occurrence chance as below:

● Facility management benefit to office workplace

In private organizations, when the firm has facility management department, whether it can bring efficient administration to influence clerks to work efficiently in office, e.g. reducing administrative time or shortern time to work in administrative processes, in order to achieve minimizing clerk number labor cost. How to design office facilities to let office staffs to feel comfortable to work and reducing their pressure to work. It seems that office working environment will influence office staff individual performance. If the office workin environment could improve efficiency and creativity of services to satisfy office workers' comfortable working environment needs. It will reduce every administration manager's working pressuse when he/she needs often to find methods to attempt to encourage whose administrative clerks to avoid to waste working time to do some non-major administration tasks.

Hence, how to design or allocate or arrange office any facilities' stored locations or whether how many equipment number is the enough to store in the locations, which will influence office employees' working attitude in order to raise or reduce their administration tasks efficiency indirectly, e.g. the office is clean or dirty, whether office reception has enough information telephone switchboard operation facilities, whether every clerk's table has enough computers number to supply to every to use, whether internet speed is fast or slow in order to let any employees can send and receive email to communicate or download any document from internet in short time, whether data processing and computer system maintenance service supply is enough to be repaired to employees' computers immediately when their computers are broken to wait repaire, whether website editing facilties operation whether is enough to link to office every staffs in order to let any office staffs can apply internet to do their tasks conveniently in short time.

Hence, all of these general office equipment facilities whether they are enough supplied and their stored positions anywhere are the suitable to assist any clerks to work conveniently, they will influence every office employee's administrative and productive efficiency indirectly as well as all faxs, copying machines, computers, whether internet linking maintenance service time is short or long to prepare to any office employees to use conveniently any time, these different issues will also influence every employee individual efficiency in office. Hence, it concludes that office working environment, facilities supply number, facilities maintenance service and facilities location storing both factors will influence employee individual administrative productive efficieny in office.

● facility management benefits to service working environment

Can effective facility management improve service working environment to raise employee individual work performance? It is a concern about the quality of service to its customer question. The term" standards and goals" are often used to measure staff individual service performance whether he/she can serve to customers to let them to feel this staff's service performance or attitude is good or bad.

Is the service workplace working environment facilities enough, it will influence customer service staff individual performance.

For shopping center service industry case example, for this suitation, e.g. shopping center's facilities are enough or are placed to the suitable locations in order to let the shopping center's customers to feel comfortable to shopping when they enter this shopping center as well as whether the shopping center's facilities can influence the customer service staffs to serve whose shopping customers easily or difficult, due to whether the shopping center's facilities whether are adequate supplied or their locations are the best suitable positions to influence their service performance to let them to feel easier or comfortable to serve their customers in any large size shopping centers. For example, whether the lamps' lighting energy is enough to let the shoppers to feel safe to walk to visit any shops when there are many shoppers were walking to cause crowd and they feel diffuclt to walk to avoid any body contact to any one in busy time when the shopping center has no enough lights to let them to see anywhere in the shopping center's dark environment. Then it will influence customer service staffs to feel difficult to find any shopping center customers, e.g. when two shopping center customers are fighting in one location where is far away to the shopping customer service staffs and securities in the shopping center, because the shopping center is large and it has no enough light to let the customer service staffs and securities to find their frighting location to deal their fighing behavior and other shopping center's shoppers will feel very dangerous to walk their fighting location to avoid to close them. Then, it will has possible to cause death or hurt to any one of these two fighting shoppers ,even other shoppers' lifes. Because the shopping center's securities and customer service staffs who need to spend much time to find their fighting location, it will delay they can bring the policemen to their fighting location when they arrive this shopping center's destination in short time in order to solve their fighting behavior to influence all shoppers' lifes in this shopping center. Hence, the shopping center whether it has enough lamps number and the lamps' light whether is enough, these lighting facilities will influence any shopping center customer service staffs and securities who can spend less time to arrive any locations to deal any urgent matters.

For another suitation in shopping center, if the shopping center has no enough paying telephone service facilities to supply shoppers to phone to anyone when they feel need to phone to any in the shopping center. Then, it will lead to some shoppers decide to find where the shopping center's receiption's telephone to supply to them to phone call to anyone. If ther are ten shoppers are waiting to use the shopping center's receiption's telephone to phone call to their friend or family within one minute. Thus, it will influence the reception customer service staffs feel difficult to arrange how to distribute the only one telephone to these ten shoppers to use to phone call their friend or family when they are queuing within their one minute waiting time in the shopping center's reception. If these ten shoppers can not use the receiption telephone to phone call anyone. hen, they will feel disatisfactory and complain to the reception service staffs unpolitely. So, lacking enough facilities in the shopping center's any where, it will possible to influence their shopping centers' shoppers to feel all shopping center's service staff individual performance to be poor. It means that if the shopping center expects to improve customer satisfaction to its customer service staff's behavioral performance, it meets have enough facilities to be supplied in the shopping center to let its shoppers to feel it is one comfortable and safe shopping center. In conclusion, shopping center's facilities will have possible to influence shoppers' feeling to evaluate its customer service staffs to evaluate whether their service attitudes are good or poor indirectly.

● Can facility management improve productivity

The productivity means resources (input) is therefore the amount of products or services (output), which is produced by them. Hence, higher (improved) productivity means that more is produced with the same expectton of resource, i.e. at the same cost is terms of land materials, machine, time or labor. Alternatively, it means same amount is produced at less labor cost in term sof land, material, machine, time for labor that is utilized. So, it brings this question: How can facility management improve productivity? I shall explain as these several aspects, it is possible to be improved productivity from (FM) successfully.

Improved productivity of farm land: If the farming land has better facility management to bring advantages by using better seed, better facilities of cultivation and most fertilizer. It is in the agricultural sense is increased (improved). So, facility management can bring benefits to any land resource to raise productivity in possible. It implies that the productivity of land used for better facility management of industrial purposes is said to have been increased if the output of products or service within that area of industrial land is increased output aim.

Improved productivity of material: If the factory has improved better equipment by facility management method to assist skillful workers to raise the manufacture cloth number, then the productivity of the cloth number is improved by (FM) method.

Improved productivity of labour: When the factory has good manufacturing equipment facilities to be supplied to improve methods of work to product more producing number per hour, then (FM) improved productivity of worker. Hence, in any workplaces, when organization has good facilities, it will influence employees to raise productivities in possible, because they need often to improved equipment facilties manufacture products to achieve higher producton number aim.

● Can facility management raise bank employee
productivity

Bank workplace environment is busy, the bank counter service staffs need to contact many bank clients to help them to serve or withdraw money from bank's counters. Whether does the quality of environment in bank workpace will influence the determination level of employee's motivation, subsequent performance productivity in bank working environment. For example, if the bnk's staffs need work under inconvenient conditions , it will bring low performance and face occupatinal health diseases causing high abenteeism and turnover.

In general, bank size is usually small, it will have many bank clients enter bank to contact counter staffs to need them to help them to save or withdraw money. So, it will bring air pollution the crowd queue in every bank counter challenge when the bank has many people are queue waiting in counters to queue. So, bank working condition problem relates to environmental and physical factors which will influence every bank counter staff individual working performance to serve bank clients satisfactory. However, bank staffs need to deal many documents concern every client personal data every day. So, they need to spend much time to use computer and painting machines. This is particularly true for these employees who spend most of the day operating a computer terminal in bank workplace. As more and more computers are being installed in workplaces, an increasing number of business has been adopting designs for bank offices installment. So, bank needs have effective facilities management design because of demand of bank staffs for more human comfort.

An good equipment facility management for bank staffs to use conveniently, it is assumed that better workplace environment can motives bank employees and produces better productivity. Hence, bank office environment can be described in terms of physical and behavioral components to influence bank staffs to work inefficiently. To achieve high level of abnk employee productivity, bank organizations must ensure that the physical environment in conductive to bank different department organizational needs, facilitating interaction and privacy, formality and informality, functionalit and disciplinarily, e.g. house loan or private loan departmets, counter service department, visa card application department. Thus, in a high safe privary facility management working environment will let different department bank staffs feel safe to worry about privacy loss in possible. So, the improving bank facility to bring safe and high privacy to avoid bank client individual loss in working environment issue, the facility management can be results to bring these benefits, such as in a reduction in a number of complaints and absenteeism and an increase in productivity.

● Can (FM) create value to organization?

(FM) can reduce managing facilties as a strategic resource to add value to the organization and its overall performance, e.g. saving the energy in building and take care of shuttle buses and parking facilities space management for brikes, on economic efficiency and effectiveness, or good price and value for the organization.

If the organization expects to apply (FM) process to save energy, it depends on possible input factors, i.e. interventions in the accommodation facilities services. So, it seems that the organization expects to save its energy consumption in its building. It needs have goos space management facilities between parking its shuttle buses and brikes in its property's car park.

Why does space facility management is important to influence efficiency and productivity. For one school's building example, when the school decides none of the two gymnasiums student sport entertainment centers to be built in order to reduce financial cost and higher benefits. Remarkably, the use of space with the school overall strategic goals , such as creating spaces that better can support the teaching, motivate students and teachers, attract more students and increase the utilisation of existing space to accomodate an increasing number of students.

If it hopes to make high quality teaching facilities on student's choice where to study. The school will need to choose to build either one comfortable and new design facility teaching accommodation or build two gymnasium sport entertainment centers in its limited land space either for students' learning or sport aim. Due to it feels new teaching accommodcation can make more attractive to increase students numbers to choose it to study more than building two new gymnasusm sport centers to let them do sport in school.

Hence, space choise (FC) management strategy will be one important considerable issue, when the organization has limited land space resources to make choose to build any constructions in order to increase many clients number. Such as the school organization has limited stortage land resource to let it to build either two gymnasium sport entertainment centers or one new teaching accommodation in order to attract many students to choose it to learn. Hence, it needs to gather data to make more accurate evaluation to decide how to apply its space facility to choose to build these both kinds of buildings in order to achieve the attractive student learning choice aim, so whether teh two sport entertainment activity centers or one new teaching accommodation choice, it needs to gater information to decide whether the school ought to choose to build which kind of building in order to achieve the increase of student number aim, so space facility management will be this school's land shortage problem.

The relationship between facility
management and consumer
behavior

How and why shop facility management can influence consumer individual shopping behavior? If it is possible, what shop facility management factors can influence their consumption decision when they enter the shop to plan to buy anything. I shall indicate some shop case studied to expline whether how and why every shop's facility management can influence consumer individual consumption desire when any one consumer enters any shops.

● Shop's low ceiling height location (FM) influcence consumer behavior

Can the shop's ceiling height influence shoppers' shopping behavior? Can the shops's variation in ceiling height can influence how consumers process information to decide to make purchase decision in the shops, e.g. for this suitation, when the consumer enters the shop, he/she feels the ceiling height is low and it has a lamp wil contact his/her head in possible. So, he/she chooses to move far away from the low ceiling beight location in the shop. It is possible that shop's ceiling low height and the lamp locates at the ceiling low height position will influence many customers' choices to leave the low ceiling height and lamp location, then the shop's low ceiling height will have possible to influenced many customers to choose to find the another shop to buy the similar kind of products , due to the lamp locates in the low ceiling height, so this lamp and low ceiling height will be possible factor to influence any shoppers who won't choose to walk to this dangerous location in the shop. If the shop's all spaces are ceiling height and it has many lamps are located at the low ceiling height spaces. Then, it will be serious to cause many shoppers do not want to spend too much time to choose any products in the shop because they feel dangerous to walk to the any low ceiling height lamps' locations in the shop.

Hence, hoe to design the different concept may be activated by the showroom ceiling if it were relatively high, as it tends to be in mall stores, versus low, as it is in most strip mall shops and outlet centers. Relatively high ceilings may bring safe shopping emotion to let any consumers to feel thoughts related to freedom, whereas lower ceilings may let consumers to feel dangerous to walk the locations in any shops. Hence it seems any shops ought not neglect whether their ceiling height is tall and the lamps ought avoid to locate in any low ceiling height locations in order to influence consumers number to be decreased.

● Can house facility management influence consumer individual purchase intention?

When one new property is built, whether the property consumers will consider how the new property is facilited to influence their purchase intention to the property will the new property's (FM) influence buyers in real estate markets' preferences choice and living interest. Any new property's internal characteristics of the house unit itsel , such as rooms available, when example, of external are location, accessibility to utilities services and facilities will have possible to influence the property buyer's final property purchase decision, so it seems that even the property price is cheap, it is not represent the property buyer will choose to buy the property, if he/she feels the property's facility mangement is poorer to compare other similar kinds of properties.

So, it can help real estate analysts better explain and predict the behavior of decision makers in real estate markets. Property consumers will search for property information, concerns the property's quality, price distinctiveness, ability, facility mangement, service of the property's external environment to decide whether the property is high value to choose to buy to compare other kinds of properties.

However, the external environmental forces, such as limited resources, e.g. time or financial will influence whose property consumption choice and living the property's satisfaction feeling (represent) a feedback machanism from post-property purchase reflection used to inform subsequent decisions. The process of the property buyer's leaving experience will serve to influence the extent to which the property consumer how to consider future next time property purchases decision and new information methods. Hence, when one property consumer chooses to buy a house, it refers house features ar house internal attributes , such as quality of building, the design as well as internal and external design, which are important factors for a property consumer when he/she needs to select and purchases one house.

The other (FM) factors which can influence the property consumers' needs, include living space as features, such as the size of kitchen, bathroom, bedroom, living bath and other rooms available in the house. The environment of housing area is also important factor, e.g. the condition of the neighbourhood, attractiveness of the area, quality of neighbouring houses, type of neighbouring houses, type of neighbouring houses, density of housing, wooded area or free coverage, slope of the attractive views, open space, non-residential uses in the areas vacant sites, traffic noise, level of owner-occupation in neighbourhoos, level of education in neighbourhood level of income in neighbourhood, security from crime, quality of schools, religious of neighbourhood, transportation , shopping center, sport entertainment can be supplied to close to the house area. All these human related issue of the property's location will also influence the property buyer's living location selection. Hence, above (FM) influence property consumer purchase behavior, it is based on the relationship behavior. The consumer's house purchase intention and house features, living space, environment and distance to recreation center, supermarket, library etc. public facilities variable (FM) factors.

In conclusion, the house internal space facility management and external environment facility management factors will influence property consumer individual house purchase intention.

● The effects of in-store shelf design facility management factor influences consumer behavior

Can every store retailer's shelf design influence supermarket and large retail stores shoppers' behaviors when they visit the stores? However, currently many stores tend to build on traditional and repetitive design for their store shelf layout, it brings results in outdated store layouts.

Another important store shelf layout design aspect, retailer should consider carefully is the allocation of products on shelves. So, it seems that efficienct shelf space allocation management does not only minimize the economic threats of empty product shelves, it can also lead to higher consumer satisfaction, a better customer relationship.

Why does supermarket shelves design is important? Any retail tore will sell product category within a shelf. They can use the same nominal category , e.g. negular crisps next to light crisps, same food prouct shelf. Anyway, a goal-based shelf display can contain several product, that determine a common consumer goal, e.g. fair trade. Hence, these two categorical product structuring methods are also described in terms of how to put product, or food on shelf benefit and attribute -based product categories.

These shelf design food or product storing method will have more influence consumers to choose to buy the supermarket or retail store food or products more easily , due to products, or food put on their shelf very convenient and systematic to attract consumers' shopping consideration to the supemarket or retail store.

● Music (FM) environment influence consumer consumption desire

Is it possible that shop music (FM) environment can raise consumer purchase desire? In one shop or supermarket, it can provide soft music (FM) equipment to let consumers can listen soft music or songs in the supermarket or retail shop when the are staying to spend more time shopping and whether soft music facility can be expected to raise customer individual value-added options to the music facility shop in the supermarket ot retail shop.

Can the music facilities prolong consumers to stay in the store? It is possible that tempo soft music can influence consumers to stay longer time in restaurants and supermarkets and retail shops. It is possible that the different types of music (FM) in any supemarket, restaurant, retail shop owning music listening facility shopping environment. It will have possible to influence consumers to prolong staying in their shops. For example, one wine selling retail shop has classical music (FM) listening equipment to let consumers to listen when they enter the wine shop, it is possible to cause consumers to choose to buy more expensive wine products. Some researchers indicate when the wine shop owns classical music facility to let all consumers can list classical music when they walk in the wine ship, it can evoke the wine consumers to choose to buy purchasing higher prices wine products in the long term classical music listening environment. Otherwise, in a fitness sport center, musical fir and excite or popular music (FM) environment can attract fitness sport players' emotion to play and kind of fitness sport facility longer time. Also, in one supermarket, the soft music facilities listening environment can persuade or attract food consumers to spend more time in the mall consuming food or beverage also purchase othe products more easily, due to they will listen soft music to be influenced to choose to prolong staying time in the supermarket. It seems that it has relationship between retail shop's music facility environment and consumer's emotion will be influenced by these different kinds of soft music or songs to raise consumption desire in the supermarket, if some consumers like to proplong to stay longer consuming time in the owning music facility environment's retail shop.

In fact, some researchers indicate the owning background music facility selling environment's ship , it can affect consumer decision making, memory, concentration consumption desire. So, classical , jazz soft music facility ought be installed in restaurants, retail shops, restaurants' environment. Otherwise, popular , exciting, noise, pop music facilty ought be installed in fitness sport centers, theme park entertainment parks business places in order to influence fitness sport players or theme park entertainers to prolong playing or entertaining time to feel real sport or entertainment theme park playing machine facility's entertainment enjoyable feeling as well as attracting restaurant or supermarket or retail shop's consumers to proplong their staying time to make consumption decisions. Hence, it seems that music facility environment can raise consumers' consumption desire in possible.

● University bookstore atmospheric factors how to influence student's purchase book behavior?

Any university bookstore how to do international control and structuring of book internal environment to raise students' purchase book desires in university itself school's bookstore, it will be one popular question to any universities. Hence, whether the university bookstore internal (FM) factors include: lighting, music, colors, scents, temperature, layout and general cleanliness as well as university external factors include: the university bookstore shape/size, windows, university parking facility for students availability and location,which can play an influential role of the university bookstore image in order to influence the university itself students to choose to buy books from themselves bookstore or university outside bookstores.

Whether the university student needs to spend how long individual learning time and how mcuh learning nervous to spend time to choose any kinds of book in the univeristy bookstore or outside bookstores, this issue , he/she will consider. Because he/she does want to expect spend much time and nervous to choose to buy books in any bookstore. If the universitt's bookstore physical location and internal (FM) desing image can let its target student customers to feel it's all book products are stored in any attractive internal book shelves places, e.g. the cheapest and the most expensive different subjects of text books are stored in one system method to bring the positive image of value snd quality in order to let university target student customers can find their books' choice location to spend less time to search any books to read in the unviersity bookstore easily.

However, due to learning time is shortage to every university student of the universty's book shelves can display all text books in the attractive right locations in the university bookstore as well as the university's bookstore ought has an adequate space to let university students to walk to anywhere and find any subjects of text books and compare their book sale prices in the bookstore's any shelves' locations easily when they walk to the subject of book shelf location, then they can make accurate decision either to buy the right kind of subject book or not buy it to read in the short time. They will ferl their book choice purchase decision making process won't influence their learning time in themselves univeristy. Then, the university students will be influenced by themselve university's bookstore's attractive external university facilites in the univeristy's any teaching places and the university's bookstore internal attractive environment facility image which can influence the students to make final choices to buy their liking books to read from their university's itself bookstore. Hence, the university's bookstore internal and external building environment (FM) design factors will influence its students whether choose to buy from themselves bookstore or another outside general bookstore.

● How and why does retail atmospheric environment influence consumers behavior in retail shop?

Any shop's internal facility management design can influence atmospheric environment to influence consumer individual shopping desire, e.g. colour, lighting, music, crowding, design and layout factors, which internal shop (FM) environment can influence the first time shopping visiting client ' cognitive process how to feel the shop store image. Such as if the store's (FM) environment can bring enjoyable and fun and happy image to let them to feel shopping's enjoyment.

In conclusion, when consumers will like to stay longer time in the store. Due to the store's internal (FM) atmospheric environment can attract them to stay longer time in the store. Then, the customer's shopping value will raise and it can bring purchasing intention and shopping satisfaction. How can (FM) influence retail atmospheric physical (FM) environment ? Can (FM) bring indirect relationship to influence how the consumer individual causes positive or negative purchase intention when he/she has influence to proplong staying desire in the store, when the shop has good (FM) , it will bring long time to make consumption chance in the shop.

Chapter 3
MTR (UNDERGROUND TRAIN) TRANSPORTATION FACILITY

MANAGEMENT

● Why MTR underground train transportation needs to know passenger behaviour

Understanding individual passenger behaviour is essential for the design MTR transportation, because who can choose to catch bus, taxi, tram, train ferry etc. different kinds of public transportation tools. Individual traveler who decides to catch which kinds of public transportation tools, it depends on whether the public transportation tool can provide real time travel information, liking link travel time schedule. So, MTR underground train needs to understand where it has terminal to give convenience to the local living areas of time travelers to choose to catch MTR easily. Although, MTR ticket fare is one factor to influence any passengers choice. But, those other factors can also influence them to choice. e.g. MTR any terminal location of convenience, short time travelling, none crowding in busy (peak) time, MTR platform waiting arrival time, none sudden MTR engineering machines broken accident events occurrence frequently etc. different factors, any one of these factors which can influence passengers who choose to catch MTR or other kinds of transportation tools.

● Why route choice can influence passenger behavioural choice

Usually, the busy time passengers will regard the route choice as a coordination problem to influence them to choose to catch which kinds of transportation tools. The route choice is as an opportunity costs to influence any busy time passengers to decide to choose to catch which kind of transportation tool which is the best right choice in the right time among of them. In the short time, for example, it seems any busy time passengers will choose to catch bus to substitute MTR underground train transportation tool, due to who feels the bus can arrive any destinations to compare other kinds of transportation tools in the most short time. However even if the MTR can either charge cheaper ticket fare to sell full day or charge discount ticket fare to sell in the busy (peak) time to compare to bus fare. It is possible that the busy time passengers will still choose to catch bus, if between the bus terminal and the another bus terminal that distance is the shorter time route to spend time to arrive destination to compare between the MTR terminal to the another MTR terminal arrival time . Also, although the busy time passengers will feel to enounter traffic jam to influence sitting or waiting bus time to be longer time in possible and who also feel MTR can avoid traffic jam problem. However, usually any busy (peak) time passengers will feel the chance of traffic jam occurrence will be less. So, the short bus route choice is more potential factor to influence the busy (peak) time passengers still to choose bus to catch.

However, if anyone wants to investigate results of day-to-day route choice which can be transferred to more realistic environment. It is necessary to explore individual behaviour in an interactive experimental set up to ensure busy (peak) time passenger transportation behavioural choice. For example, a passenger has a choice between a main road (M) and a side road (S) for travelling from (A) to (B). (M) is faster if (M) and (S) are chose by the same number of passengers. So, this method can be researched whether MTR terminal station is located at the main road (M) or the side road (S) where is more suitable to accept to passengers generally.

● Why trip time reliability and crowding factors can influence MTR passenger choice.

Other problem is MTR busy (peak) time's crowding in public transportation occurrence of MTR underground train transportation tool is becoming a growth to concern as MTR demand growth at a busy (peak) time. To capture the MTR passengers benefits with reduced crowding from improved MTR public transport service and image. It is necessary a identify the relevant dimensions of crowding that are meaningful measures of what crowding means to MTR passengers. Two main influences on MTR model choice that are growing in relevance are trip time reliability and crowding. It represents a benefit-cost framework. In fact, MTR passengers can be willing to pay more expensive ticket fare, it MTR can avoid crowding and short and the accurate arrival trip time between terminals is reliable to occur. How to measure of MTR crowding, e.g. weighting the gap between the busy time, the standard (i.e. objective) and the perceived (i.e. subjective) metrics. We are not in a position to definitely map the two dimensions, which is a crucial requirement for translating objective improvements into equivalent subjective gains that then can be applied, willingness to pay estimates MTR ticket fares to obtain the additional MTR passenger benefits of MTR public transportation investment to any terminal stations. Because MTR crowding has a negative impact on passengers in terms of psychological on emotional distress. MTR passengers are willing to stand for up to 20 minutes of the service is fast and reliable. However crowding outweighed these benefits from a MTR passenger's perpective, experienced crowding leads a increased dissatisfaction. e.g. stress and less privacy during who needs to stand up in MTR. Due to there are no enough places to supply to them to stand up in MTR. If the MTR trip time was longer time between the passenger's terminals, who will feel more dissatisfaction and it will cause who feels whether who ought need to choose to catch other transportation tools to substitute MTR next time. e.g. bus, train, tram, ferry, taxi etc. So, from an operator's perspective, the MTR service frequency or MTR size is significantly influenced by the level of ridership, which sends a signal to respond if the monitored crowding level exceeds the benchmark standard in the busy time. e.g. in the morning time or at the night time, the students or employment people who need to go to schools or offices (working places). The locations of different places between MTR terminals and crowding are regarded as a key service attribute for MTR pubic transportation along with other factors, such as travelling time and reliability, e.g. service quality, none engineering machines are broken to cause MTR stops suddenly.

Given the increasing importance of crowding on both the disutility to existing MTR public transportation users and the influence to it. MTR passenger can choose to use either the MTR public public transportation or other public transportation. It is timely to review the MTR current measures of crowding defined by transportation authorities. MTR operators ought evaluate whether they apporpriately reflect MTR each traveler experiences and perceptions of crowding in busy (peak) time. I suggest that MTR needs to buy other underground trains to supply to the busy (peak) time passengers to let them have enough seats to sit down, so who do not need to stand up in any MTR underground trains when they catch MTR underground trains in busy time. It aims to let who are willingness to pay the estimation of reasonable ticket fares to compare the other kinds of transportation tools in the busy (peak) time.

● What is the crowding difference between train and MTR underground train.
In fact, crowding won't be happened to brother these transportation tools easily in the busy time and non busy time both. e.g. bus, taxi, train, tram, ferry. Because passengers can not choose to stand up in these transportation tools easily, due to these transportation tools have no enough areas (spaces) to let them to stand up easily . So, the crowding will be avoided to occur in these tranportation tools usually. Otherwise, MTR will have many passengers who can choose to stand up because MTR design of length is very long and it has enough areas (places) to let passengers to choose to stand up, even there have none any seats are provided to let them to sit down. So, MTR passengers will feel more dissatisfaction and crowding easily, especial in any peak (busy) time every day.

Comparing to bus, much more diverse crowding measures are defined in the passenger rail industry. For passenger, different specifications for measuring crowding are found across countries and even within a country. For example, rail crowding measures in the UK, the passengers in excess of capacity is crowding measure that applies to all London and South east operators weekday train services at a London terminus during the morning peak from 0700 to 09: 59 , and those departing during the afternoon peak from 16:00 to 18:59 (office of rail regulation 2011 year). The overall PIXC figure is considered the planned standard class capacity of each train service as well as the actual number of standard class passengers on the service at the critical point. i.e. the location on a trains of standard class passengers that surpass the planned capacity as the difference between the number of actual passengers and the capacity of the train divided by the number of passenger is within the capacity . So, it seems train and MTR underground public transportaton tools had been encountering the crowding problems in peak time, the difference in train passengers need to wait next train or more train arrival is who doesn't plan to enter the train, when who discovers the current train has no seats to provide to them to sit down in whose trip. Otherwise, MTR passengers can choose either to stand up within the large areas (places) if who discovered there are no any seats to provide to them to sit down or who can wait the next MTR arrival in order to who can sit down. It seems MTR transportation tool crowding environment includes in waiting platform and inside of the MTR underground train. Otherwise, train transportation tool crowding environment only includes the waiting platform and the passengers will not have crowding feeling inside of the train, due to none of passengers choose to stand up inside any trains because any train inside has no enough places to let them to stand up.

● How MTR can attract many passengers.

On the commuter departure time choice of any reference point researching hand, the departure time decisions of communters are of fundamental importance of peak period MTR traffic congestion. However, whether on the demand side, MTR underground train congestion relief measures, such as MTR ticket fare to every terminal station needs to be charged cheaper fare or discount fare in the peak (busy) time every day. To aim to attract many passengers to choose to catch MTR Underground train public transportation tools, substitute to choose other public transportation tools in the peak time.

Over the past decades, there have been very active research efforts in the departure time problem, both in econometric modeling and dynamic user equilibrium fields. Although, these works provide valuable insights into dynamic commuter decision making, they do not identify the commuters' response to gains and losses related to whole actual arrival time to reference points who may have relative. The appliability of the reference point hypothesis of prospect theory to the commuter's departure time decision making to obtain a better understanding of how departure time choice in MTR platform during their waiting underground train arrival time. However, every MTR underground train actual arrival time and deviation variables related to reference points (gains and losses) are the key factors in the departure time choice model. How the MTR underground train of every commuter's daily departure time decision can be modelled when the reference point hypothesis of prospect theory. The MTR underground train's schedule delay is defined as the difference between the preferred arrival time (PAT) and the actual arrival time (AT) for a given MTR commuter. In a daily MTR commute, a commuter in the indifference band actual arrival time is an essential feature of MTR schedule study. Two reference points are the earliest acceptable arrival time and the work starting time for a given MTR platform waiting passengers. In psychological view point, prospect theory proposes that the displeasure of a loss is perceived or greater than the pleasure of a gain of the same attitude and therefore, the value function is stronger for losses than gains.

To conclude, it seems that if MTR waiting passengers need not spend long time to wait underground train arrival in platform and it can provide seats to let them to sit down in the busy (peak) crowding time. It will make them to feel pleasure, even the MTR ticket fare is not fair and reasonable to charge higher fare to compare other kinds of public transportation tools fares. So the peak waiting time factor can influence the passengers to choose other kind of transportation tools to catch easily. Moreover, MTR's two reference points are the earliest role. Similarly a loss is observed when the MTR platform waiting commuter experiences or actual arrival time which is beyond that the MTR schedule time. Due to that a MTR waiting commuter is as an early side arrival of whose actual arrival time is earlier than whose preferred arrival time.

CHAPTER VI

Facility management how influences airport and logistic employee performance

Facility management influences airport and logistic employee performance
● Facility management assists employees reduce
maintenance service expenditure
Facility management provides a variety of non core operations and maintenance services to support any organizations' operation. For logistic organization example, it is possible to provide effective maintenance service to warehouse in order to reduce warehouse facilities to be damaged to bring to spend to buy any new equipment facilities expenditure. So, when the logistic company's warehouse facilities can be maintenance to be the best quality. Then, they can be used these warehouses' machines facilities again. Their performance can assist workers to manufacture any products to keep the most efficiently an raising the best production performance in whole manufacturing process. Then, this logistic company's facility management department can bring to avoid purchase any new machine facilities expenditure spending. One to these warehouses' production machine facilities are kept in the best production performance environment even in long term production need.

I shall indicates airport and warehouse facilities how to influence employees performances as below:

(1) How can comfortable warehouse facilities influence workers' efficiencies in logistic industry ?
The logistic industry's facility management department can create cost savings and efficiency of the warehouse's workplaces. It's machines facilities (production machines) are dealt with the maintenance management of the physical assets maintenance service. FM (facilities management) has been being applied to industrial facilities in logistic and warehouse industry long term as well as maintenance plays a significant role to ensure the full service and the warehousing system, including both building components and equipment in warehouse.
Maintenance service is needed to bring a certain level of availability and reliability of a warehouse facilities system and its components and its ability

perform to a standard level of quality. So , it seems that logistic industry's warehouse asset cost reducing. It depends on whether it has one facility management department to provide maintenance service to itself warehouse workplace's production machine facilities and warehouse building itself in order to let workers t feel the manufacturing machines can bring good manufacturing performance to assist them to produce any products in one safe warehouse workplace environment. Hence, the performance measurement of warehouse maintenance issue will be valued to be consider to every warehouse manager and facility manager in logistic industry.

In logistic industry, (FM) works at two level on the one hand, it provides a safe and efficient working environment, which is essential to influence warehouse workers whether how they perform to do their manufacturing tasks or logistic goods delivery tasks in warehouse. When they feel the warehouse is safe environment to work. They will not need to consider anywhere has risk to cause they die by accident in warehouse. Hence, they can concentrate on doing their every tasks . On the other hand, it can involve strategic issues, such as property (warehouse workplace and management, strategy property decision and warehouse facility, e.g. manufacturing machine, facility maintenance and checking planning and maintenance planning development.

However, reducing the operating expense issue will be the main aim when the logistic company feels that it has need to set up one in-house facility management department to carry on any maintenance service for its warehouses' any workplace property and manufacturing machines facilities. So, when the logistic company decides to implement one facility management department, it needs to ensure its facility management department can bring the minimum level of keeping manufacturing performance and efficiency to its warehouses' any manufacturing machines and warehouses' property to avoid to be damaged in short term, such as loss of business due to failure in service, provision of project to customer satisfaction, provision of safe environment, effective utilisation of workplace space, e.g. warehouse effectiveness and communication between the workers and the logistic managers in the warehouse workplace , due to the warehouse's space is not enough maintenance service reliability to the logistic company's warehouse, responsiveness of the warehouse's worker individual negative emotion problem, due to he/she often feels need to work in one unsafe warehouse working environment. Hence, it seems that poor or unsafe warehouse working environment can influence workers feel negative emotion to work to bring low efficiency (inefficiency) or under productive performance in warehouse. It has relationship to influence they to bring psychological negative emotion feeling to work when the organization lacks one effective warehouse management repairing service to be provided to the warehouse's facilities and properties' maintenance needs in order to avoid ineffective measurement and misleading of performance.

Hence, the logistic company's facilities management department often needs to be reviewed whether its maintenance service level is passed to achieve the lowest repair (maintenance) service standard to its warehouse itself property and manufacturing machine or warehouse delivery tool facilities or warehouse lamps' light whether is enough to let workers to see anything clearly to avoid accident occurrence or see anything to work clearly or the warehouse space areas are enough to let they can have enough space to walk or communicate to their team supervisors or deliver any goods more easily in the short distance between the worker's sending goods location and the delivering goods destination in order to avoid because the lacking enough space to cause the accident occurrence , due to the space is not enough to let they deliver their goods to any locations in warehouse.

Hence, it seems logistic company's (FM) department can contribute to the organization's mission, such as avoiding warehouse accident occurrence, inefficiency, not enough and unavailability of the facility for future needs when the warehouse lacks enough space areas to bring poor performance of facility and dangerous warehouse itself property in warehouse, e.g. safe and reliable operations of material handling equipment and maintenance of warehouse facilities, grounds, security system, utilities, plumbing, heating , enough lighting system, air conditioning, warming heater, fire protection, security system alarm etc. facilities in warehouse.

Hence, it seems that if the logistic company expected to reduce to spend lot of excessive manufacturing machine purchase expenditure, lose of workers' life or bring workplace accidents , due to poor warehouse workplace environment, even bringing lawsuit compensation claim loss , due to the worker individual accident or death is caused from the poor warehouse facilities, or bring negative emotion to let the workers feel they are working in unsafe warehouse workplace environment. Then, it ought choose to set up on facility management department in order to provide enough maintenance service to its warehouse to avoid these non essential expenditure causing , due to these poor warehouse facilities factors.

Hence any logistic company ought choose to set up one itself in -house facility management department, it be better than outsourcing its all facilities service to one facility management (maintenance service provider) to help it to deal any kinds of maintenance service in warehouse. Because it is long term maintenance need to its warehouse's any machines and warehouse itself properties. If it chose to find one outsourcing facilitiy management maintenance service provider to replace its in-house facility management department to deal all related facilities maintenance tasks in warehouse. Then, it is possible that it needs to pay long time facilities maintenance service fee to its outsourcing facility management maintenance service provider more than itself facility management maintenance service provision department.

(2) Can facility management influence tourism industry's human resource management influence to improve productivity in airline, travel agent, hotel tourism sectors?

In tourism industry, measuring productivity froma HRM prespective is extremely difficult and has proven to be a limitation within the tourism sector. Due to the customers are not tangible. For example, how can the travel agent measure its travel consultant individual service performance to evaluate whether the travelling customer feels or does not feel satisfactory loyalty from his/her service? How can the airline measure its pilot , airline front-line travelling passenger service attendant indiviual service performance to evaluate whether his/her travelling passenger feels or does not feel satisfactory to whose service performance? Whether airport facility management can influence airline counter service staffs performance ?

However, the complaint number whether it is more or less to the airline or travel agent's service behavior , it does not represent whose service attitude or behavior or performance is poor absolutely because there are many travelling consumers whose complaints are unreasonable , although they feel satisfactory to the airline attendent or airline front -line service staffs individual service performance, but if they feel unhappy to be caused by the airline or travel agent service staff. They will still compain their performance. For this suitation example , it is possible that the travelling passenger is delayed to catch the airplance to fly, due to the country's sudden worse weather influnce, he/she will complain the airline fron-line counter travelling customer service staffs, it concerns when the air plane will arrive the airport, if the airline counter service staff's feedback is that the airplane needs long time arrival. Then, the travelling passengers will complain to the airline counter service staffs in angry. But in fact, the air plane delays to arrive the airport, the airline counter service staffs ought not need responsibilitie to explain the reason why they can not assist the delayed air plane to arrive the country in easier. Furthermore, thy will be complained unreasonably. Hence, it is difficult to measure tourism sector's service staffs ' performance, also the complaint exact number is not one judgement factor to measure their service performance absolutely.

I assume any tourism industry's front -line service airline staffs, they must attempt to serve their travelling passenger in positive service attitude and behavior. So, any tourism industy, how to improve their front -line service staff performance in order to let they to know how to deal unreasonable complaints in sudden unpredictive suitation. Their training materials or contents my include: Teaching them how to provide positive feedback to treat any travelling passenger individual difficult problems or unreasonable complaints in order to reduce their psychological pressure to unknown how to treat these passenger individual related problems when they are facing in airports or travelling agent workplaces. The travelling agent or airline travelling service organizations can attempt to collect measures of employee performance from customers , for example, comment cards in hotel rooms, airplane, travel agent's workplace, mystery shoppers etc. more focus shouls be pleased on this form of evaluation. In order to evaluate the actually place value on the customer ratings to every employee. The all every day, the form of evaluation concerning the actually value on the customer ratings , will be gathered to strategic , it has how many customers feel good or bad ratings to every employee individual performance when every one's tasks are finishing. Due to one month, it can make statistic report to calculate how much performance marks to give to every employee in order to evaluate whether every one's performance is satisfactory to be accempted to the lowest level. If the employee's marks rating is low, his/her department manager can arrange a time and day to meet him/her to discuss whether which aspects of problems who feels in order to give recommendation how to improve his/her service attitude to let customer to give higher marks rating to him/her next time.

Hence tourism industry's service sector organizations need to have one training department to arrange courses how to improve employee service performance in order to let customer to give higher marks rating to very one as well as finding methods how to excite every front line service employee individual loyalty , they can increase their confidence to know how to deal sudden unreasonable complaints in effective and efficient positive attitude. In conclusion, how to improve employee service performance issue will be any tourism service organization's HRM concerning problem. Airports need to arrange how to implement efficient and comfortable and available convenient airport facilities to let any airline service counter staffs feel enjoyable to serve their passengers. They need to know how to find the most effective methods to solve how improvement of front line employee individual performance problem in order to raise the airline or travel agent's quality of service to let itself further customers to feel its service performance is better than others. So, facility management has indirect relationship to influence airport airline service staffs performances.

In conclusion, to decide whether the company ought need or not need facilities maintenance service or either set up in-house facility management department or outsource one facility management maintenance service provider. It depends on whether its organization has how many facilities are used in its workplace, how many staffs are working the workplace, how much size of its workplace, its workplace is office or warehouse or factory, how long time of its facilities' useful time etc. factors , then it can decide whether it needs or does not need one facility maintenance service department or outsourcing facility maintenance service provider to help it to deal any facilities management problem in its organization.

● Facility management role in
organization

When one company feels that it has need facility management service. It can choose to set up either in-house facility management department or seek one outsourcing facility management service provider to help it to arrange any facility management service need. However, this facility management role is only one for the organization. It concerns this question: What facility management maintenance function can bring the benefits to the organization?

It can define that all services required for the management of building and real estate to maintain and increase their value, the means of providing maintenance support, project management and user management during the building life cycle, the integration of multi-disciplinary activities within the built environment and the management of their impact upon people and the workplace. In traditional, (FM) services may include building fabric maintenance, decoration and refurbishment, plant, plumbing and drainage maintenance, air conditioning maintenance, lift and escalator maintenance , fire safety alarm and fire fighting system maintenance, minor project management. All these are hard services. Otherwise, cleaning , security, handyman services, waste disposal, recycling, pes control, grounds maintenance, internal plants. All these are soft services. Additional services, might also include: pace planning, things moving management, business risk assessment, business continuity planning, benchmarking, space management, facilities contract outsourcing service arrangement, information systems, telephony, travel booking facility utility management, meeting room arrangement services, catering services, vehicle fleet management, printing service, postal services, archiving , concierge services, reception services, health and safety advice, environmental management.

All of these services will be every organization's in-house facility soft or hard services needs. So, it explains why some large organizations feel need one effective facility management department to help them to arrange how to implement facility services efficiently in order to achieve cost reducing, raising efficiency and performance improvement aims because one effective facility management control system can influence employee individual productive effort to be raised or reduced indirectly.

However, (FM) can be selected either setting up one in-house (FM) department or outsourcing its services to one facility management service provider to help the organization to solve any kinds of facilities maintain service problems. One on-house (FM) department is a team, it needs employees to deliver all (FM) services. Some specialist services are needed to be outsourced, when the service is on expertise in the company. The no expertise services will be outsourced to simple service contracts, e.g. lift and escalator (FM) department will have direct labour, but it can outsource some specialist to help it to do some complex facilities management service. So, the team leader can of can manage whose team staffs, such as maintenance technicians run low risk operations . Otherwise, the outsourcing facility management service provider needs to help it to operate high risk operations or maintenance vital plant facility management service. Anyway, it can set up in-house (FM) department to arrange specialist direct labour and outsourced (FM) services to more than one facility management service providers to do different kinds of (FM) services. One of these outsourcing (FM) service provider, who can arrange sub-contractors to assist it to finish any (FM) services of it's outsourcing (FM) services are more complex to compare the other sub-contractors (third parties).

● What is a facility manager's role to provide quality service to satisfy its user needs?

We need to know how quality can be defined in facility management and why it should be defined by the customer? How facility managers can find out customer (user) needs? What are the difficulties in finding out users' needs and in delivering quality services? Whether improving quality always means requiring higher cost?

In general, facility manager's major responsibilities may include these major functional areas: longer range and annual facility planning, facility financial forecasting, real estate acquisition and/or disposal, work specification, installation and space management, architectural and engineering planning and design, new construction and/or renovation, maintenance and operations management, maintenance and operation management, telecommunications integration, security and general administrative services. When the facility manager had implemented any one of these FM services for those user. How does he/she provide excellent (FM) service quality ot let whose users to feel satisfactory?

In fact, quality issues can not be considered without customer-oriented perspective service quality involves a comparison of expectation with performance. (FM) service quality is a measure of how well to service level delivered matches customer expectation. So, these issues are (FM) service user's general measurement level requirement. The (FM) manager needs to achieve these the minimum performance measurement level to satisfy whose (FM) user's needs.

However, (FM) service quality has three characteristics: Intangibility, heterogeneity, inseparability. But in fact, (FM) service delivered may be through tangible physical aspects, e.g. factory plant workplace building, machine equipment maintenance, intangible (FM) services, e.g. managing space moving in plant to let staffs to work, managing outsourcing cleaners to clean factory equipment. However, all (FM) service performance often varies, due to the behavior of service personnel. Hence, a well developed job specification and training can help to improve the consistence of services of (FM). Any (FM) production and consumption of many services may are inseparable and they are usually interactions between the (FM) client and the contact person from the service provider.

Hence, it seems that service quality is considered as hard to evaluate. In (FM) service quality, it includes physical quality and interactive non-physical service quality. Physical quality is tangibles: The appearance of the physical facilities, equipment, personnel and communication materials. Non-physical services quality means reliability: The ability to perform the promised service dependably and accurately; responsiveness means the willingness to help customers and provide promopt service to let user to feel; assurance mans the competence of the system in its credibility in providing a courteous and secure service and empathy means the approachability, ease of access and effort taken to understand customers' needs.

Hence, a good performance of (FM) manager , he/she ought satisfy the user's tangible and non-tangible both service quality needs. I recommend that he/she can attempt to predict what are the (FM) customer expects in each (FM) service needs. Then, it can make decision what aspect(s) will be the (FM) users major (FM) service need and what aspect(S) won't be the (FM) users major (FM) service need. Then, he/she can make more accurate decision to arrange time, human resource , cost spending amount arrangement whether when it ought concentrate on finishing the (FM) major service tasks as well as whether how he/she ought finish the major (FM) service tasks to be more easily, e.g. how to arrange staffs number to finish, how many the minimum staffs number is needed to be arrange the major (FM) service tasks, time arrangement is important factor, because it can influence whether he/she ought finish the major (FM) service tasks today or tomorrow or later in order to have enough time to finish other non-major (FM) service tasks. Instead of time management, staff number arrangement is also important factor , if he/she arranged the excessive staffs number to do the (FM) major services tasks, then it is possible that it will have shortage of staffs number to finish the non-major (FM) service tasks on the day. So, avoiding either major or non-major (FM) services can not finish on the day. The (FM) manager needs to predict when the major (FM) services and the non-major (FM) services which are necessary to be finished in order to have enough time and staffs to assist him/her to finish every day major and non-major (FM) service effectively. Then, the achievement of his/her (FM) major and non-major tangible and non-tangible services , it will have more chance to be performed efficiently by his/her managed staffs.

In conclusion, in any organizations , (FM) manager needs have good predictable effort to evaluate whether when his/her managed team need to finish the major and/or non-major (FM) tasks as well as whether how he/she ought arrange the accurate time and staff number to finish any major and/or non-major (FM) service tasks on the day. Then, his/her leading of (FM) service team can be managed to work more efficiently in order to satisfy her/his (FM) service user's needs.

Facility management how influences
public service transport service performance
● How (FM) space moving management brings employees efficiencies
There are interesting questions: How (FM) can bring value-add to avoid loss or earn more profit to the organization? Can it influence employees to raise performance and improve efficiency ? Some organizations' (FM) service need which is necessary in order to let employees can raise productivity.
It is based on these assumptions: I assume the organizations have completely either outsourced or in-house their (FM) facility management departments will gain more effect on added value than they have no (FM) function as well as organizations have a strong coordination with the (FM) department will gain more added value than organizations with a weak coordination. Organizations in the profit aim can gain more added value than organizations in the not for profit aim sectors.
In fact, any organization is difficult to confirm it has relationship between improving performance, raising efficiency and owning (FM) function in its organization. (FM) could have to do with the attraction of easy but incomplete indicators of efficiency rather than the necessarily and less direct measures if the effectiveness and the relevance of space moving useful management, e.g. whether building has the enough space to let employees to move to work easy in order to raise efficiency, whether the building has excessive furniture and equipment number and they are putted on wrong places to be caused employees move difficulty in the building in order to influence productive performance.
However, how to arrange space moving management to equipment, e.g. copying machines, faxes, productive machines, they are putted on the locations where have enough space to let employees to move to another locations. For example, the building floor has more than 50 employees, but its space is not enough to let these 50 employees to move to any locations to let them to feel easily often. Then, it is possible to cause they

feel nervous pressure and they can feel difficult to work , when they are working in a small office space or factory space or warehouse space. Then, the consequence will be under-predictive efficiency or poor performance to any one of these 50 employees in this office or factory or warehouse.

" Facility management is responsible for coordinating all efforts related to planning, designing, and managing buildings and their systems, equipment, and furniture to enhance. The organizations abilty to compete successfully in a rapidly changing world." (F.Becker)

The author explains equipment, workplace internal space designing, furniture space putting location arrangement will have possible to influence employee individual productive performance or efficiency to be raised or reduced in the workplace. Hence, it seems that, in the value chain (FM) belongs to the activity part of the firm. To make the facilities cooperation with each office or factory or warehouse using space moving facility management. Facility space moving management must be linked strategically, tactically and operationally to other support activity to add value to the organization's office or factory or warehouse space moving management arrangement more effectively.

Thus, how to arrangement space moving management issue it will have possible to influence the organization's employee individual productive performance and efficiency in whose workplace. It seems that (FM) space moving management arrangement have indirect relationship to influence the organization's employee individual performance and efficiency , due to they need often to work in the workplace, if they feel moving difficulty , or excessive equipment , furniture number is putting into the small office, factory or warehouse locations, or they feel the office or factory or warehouse has excessive (a lot of) staffs number to work in the small space of office or factory or warehouse. Then, they can not concentrate nervous on finishing every tasks in possible. In long term, their efficiencies will be poor or inefficiencies or their performance won't be improved or causing poor performance in possible.

Instead of the not enough space moving and excessive staffs number factor, it will bring another question: Can enough information systems equipment cause a more efficient and improved performance to the organization staffs in the workplace?

I assume that the office has 100 employees and it has only ten copying machines. So it means that ten employees use one copying machine. Hence, it brings this question: Is it enough to provide only ten copying machines to average ten employees to use? It depends on other factors, e.g. whether any one of these 100 employees needs to print how many documents per day , whether the five copying machines' locations are far away to separate different locations or they are stored in one printing room in the office, whether the day has how many staffs are absent, whether the day has how many printing machine(s) is/ are broken to need to be repaired. Hence, these unpredictable external environment factors will influence whether the five copying machines number is enough to let these 100 employees to use in the office every day. Hence, facility manager ought need to spend to observe average their copying behaviors every day in order to make data record. Many employees need to use copy machines to print documents, average how many document's page number, they need to print, how much average time spending to print their documents, average how many staff absent number on the day. Even, if the all five copying machines are stored in the printing room, calculating the staffs number whether how many staffs need more than five minutes to walk to the printing room to print their documents many staffs need to spend five minute to walk to the printing room, and they have other urgent tasks to wait to finish. It is possible to influence their efficiency, due to they often need to spend more than five minutes to walk to the printing room to print documents. If there are many staffs need to often to print documents, but their printing task will have many time, e.g. 20 separate printing tasks. Then, they need to spend at least (20x5) 100 minutes to spend time to walk to the printing room to print their documents. It must influence that they should not finish the other urgent tasks on the day. If there are many staffs to spend much time to walk to the printing room in the least 20 separate printing time or more on that day. All the facility manager needs to evaluate whether all the five copy machines are stored in the printing room whether it is the best location decision or they ought need be separated to put on different office locations in their workplaces, even he/she ought need to evaluate whether it is enough copying machines number, when the office has only 5 copying machines. He/she ought need to buy more copying machines number to satisfy any one of these 100 employee individual copying task need.

In conclusion, effective office or factory or warehouse space moving facility management will be one part task of (FM) function. If the office or factory or warehouse can have accurate equipment, machine , furniture number to avoid excessive or shortage number problem to cause employees often feel moving difficult problem in their workplace when they need to move to another location to work in office or warehouse or factory as well as whether the staff needs often spend time to wait the another employee to use the copying machine to print whose document or fax machine to deliver whose document. Then, it is not that fax or printing machines number is not enough to provide the employees to use in the office or warehouse or factory workplace.

Hence, (FM) includes space moving facility management to equipment , machines, furniture number as well as choosing anywhere is(are) the suitable location (s) arrangement to putting or storing these facilities in workplace as well as decision of the staff number and the workplace area size whether it has excessive staffs number to cause these staffs need to work in the small area size of office or warehouse or factory workplace. So, the organization ought need to decide whether it needs to reduce the office's staffs number to let them to work in another more suitable locations in another workplace. Hence, all these facilities space moving management and staffs and workplace size issues will be (FM) manager's consideration issues, because these external environment factors will influence employee individual efficiency and performance to be poor to cause low valued to its organization in long term in possible .

● Predictive the choosing right
data asset and (FM) analytics
solutions to boost public
transportation service quality

Can gather the choosing right data public transportation service station facilities asset and analytics, it can give recommendation to help any organization to boost service quality? (FM) analytics data can be applied to public transportation service industry to be supported how and why the train, train, ferry , ship, air plane, underground train public transportation tools' time arrival and leaving information notice board and automated ticket paying machines facilities are putting on or stored any where locations in order to boost passengers to feel their facilities locations are convenient to let them to buy tickets and see the arrival and leaving time for the next public transportation tool from the information notice electronic board machine. So, it seems that these public transportation tools' station facilities locations can influence passengers to feel the public transportation service company how to consider to its passenger's buying ticket needs and next public transportation tool's arrival and leaving time information needs in order to boost its passengers use service quality and let them to feel better service reliable performance in any train, tram, ferry , ship, underground tram, airplane stations.

As these public transportation service organizations need to learn data analytics represent an opportunity for its ticket paying machine equipment facilities as well as the next transportation tool arrival and leaving time information notice board electronic equipment facilities anywhere the locations are the most suitable to put on or store these equipment to let passengers to walk to the ticket paying machines to buy the ticket to catch the train, tram, underground train, ferry, airplane, taxi, ship more easily. So, they do not need to spend more time to find these facilities locations and spend more time to queue to wait to buy ticket to catch the public transportation tool in stations conveniently. Instead of where is the seeking ticket paying machine location, where is the next public transportation tool arrival and leaving information notice time , these both issues will be any public transportation tool's passenger's main needs.

Hence, how to spend time to seek where the next public transportation tool's arrival and leaving time information electronic notice machine location and where the ticket paying machine location , these both factors will influence any passengers' positive or negative emotion causing. For example, if the passenger feels difficult to find the ticket paying machine in the large area size train station or /and he/she feels difficult to find the train time arrival and leaving information to let him/her to know when the next train will arrive the station. Due to he/she feels difficult to find the train ticket paying machine, he/she needs to spend much time to find any one ticket paying machine in the train station. Then, it will influence him/her to choose another public transportation tool to replace the train public transportation tool, e.g. he/she can choose to catch tram, underground train, taxi, bus, ferry, taxi, ship to replace train. So, it seems ticket paying machine and time arrival and leaving information notice electronic equipment 's location putting or stored choice will be one factor to influence the passenger to choose another kind of public transportation tool to replace train at the moment. When, he/she feels that he/she arrives the destination in the most short time. Then, the public transportation service organization (FM) manager has responsibility to evaluate whether there are enough ticket paying machines number to let passengers do not need to spend more time to queue to buy tickets to catch the public transportation tool in short time as well as there are enough time arrival and leaving for next transportation tool to let passengers to know. It will be their concerning issues when they arrive the public transportation service tool's station.

Hence, predictive passenger individual walking behavior can help the public transportation service organization to choose whether where are the most convenient and attractive locations to let the ticket paying machines and the arrival and leaving time information electronic board machines to be putted on or stored in the suitable station positions in order to let many passengers can find these essential facilities in stations very easily. So, gathering data concerns passenger walking behavior in the public transportation service any stations, which can help the facility manager to make more accurate evaluation to attempt to predict whether where the locations are common places to let passengers to choose to walk daily or where the locations are not common places to let passenger to choose not to walk daily in general. Then, he/she can apply these data of different locations in the stations to evaluate whether anywhere they will have many passengers to choose to walk or whether anywhere they won't have many passengers to choose to walk in order to make more accurate decision whether anywhere are the most suitable locations to let the ticket paying machines and the time arrival and leaving information electronic board equipment to be putter on or stored in order to let them to feel it is so easier to let them to find.

Anyway, calculating each station's passenger number per day issue is important to predict whether where , there are many passengers choose to walk or where, there are not many passengers choose to walk in these different public transportation service stations in order to evaluate whether where the stations' different ought put on paying ticket machines or time arrival and leaving information electronic boards in order to let they feel very easy to buy tickets and seeing the next arrival and leaving time information for the kind of public transportation service tool conveniently in the different stations. Moreover, if the station has no enough ticket paying machines number to be supplied to let passengers need to spend more than ten minute time to wait to buy ticket to catch the kind of public transportation service tool in every queue every day. Then it will cause them to choose another kind of public transportation tool to catch go to working place or entertainment place to replace it to on that day. Then, it will cause these passengers who often do not like to queue in the kind of public transportation service tool's any stations, who will not choose to go to anywhere of this kind of public transportation service tool's any stations again. Hence, in long term this kind of public transportation service tool will lose many passengers. Thus, calculating each station's busy time of passengers number , which can predict when it is the busy time and it can make more accurate decision whether the station has need to increase enough ticket paying machines number in order to bring enough supply number to satisfy passengers' ticket purchase need in the busy time.

In conclusion, gathering above all stations' public transportation service equipment facilities number, storing positions data and every station's passenger walking behavior data, they are necessary to any public transportation tool service industry, because these equipment number and storing locations will influence them to make decisions to choose another kind of public transportation tool to replace it's transportation service if they often feel difficult to find these facilities in its different stations. Thus, it is part of task to facility manager's responsibility if the public transportation service organization expects it won't lose many passengers , due to these external environment factor influence and it also implies cheap ticket price does not guarantee the passengers will choose to catch this kind of public transportation service tool to go to anywhere.

● The relationship between facility
management and productive
efficiency

It is one interesting question: Can facility management function bring benefits to raise productive efficiency to organizations? I shall indicate some cases to attempt to explain this possible occurrence chance as below:

● Facility management benefit to office workplace

In private organizations, when the firm has facility management department, whether it can bring efficient administration to influence clerks to work efficiently in office, e.g. reducing administrative time or shorten time to work in administrative processes, in order to achieve minimizing clerk number labor cost. How to design office facilities to let office staffs to feel comfortable to work and reducing their pressure to work. It seems that office working environment will influence office staff individual performance. If the office working environment could improve efficiency and creativity of services to satisfy office workers' comfortable working environment needs. It will reduce every administration manager's working pressure when he/she needs often to find methods to attempt to encourage whose administrative clerks to avoid to waste working time to do some non-major administration tasks.

Hence, how to design or allocate or arrange office any facilities' stored locations or whether how many equipment number is the enough to store in the locations, which will influence office employees' working attitude in order to raise or reduce their administration tasks efficiency indirectly, e.g. the office is clean or dirty, whether office reception has enough information telephone switchboard operation facilities, whether every clerk's table has enough computers number to supply to every to use, whether internet speed is fast or slow in order to let any employees can send and receive email to communicate or download any document from internet in short time, whether data processing and computer system maintenance service supply is enough to be repaired to employees' computers immediately when their computers are broken to wait repair, whether website editing facilities operation whether is enough to link to office every staffs in order to let any office staffs can apply internet to do their tasks conveniently in short time.

Hence, all of these general office equipment facilities whether they are enough supplied and their stored positions anywhere are the suitable to assist any clerks to work conveniently, they will influence every office employee's administrative and productive efficiency indirectly as well as all faxes, copying machines, computers, whether internet linking maintenance service time is short or long to prepare to any office employees to use conveniently any time, these different issues will also influence every employee individual efficiency in office. Hence, it concludes that office working environment, facilities supply number, facilities maintenance service and facilities location storing both factors will influence employee individual administrative productive efficiency in office.

● facility management benefits to service working environment

Can effective facility management improve service working environment to raise employee individual work performance? It is a concern about the quality of service to its customer question. The term" standards and goals" are often used to measure staff individual service performance whether he/she can serve to customers to let them to feel this staff's service performance or attitude is good or bad.

Is the service workplace working environment facilities enough, it will influence customer service staff individual performance.

For shopping center service industry case example, for this situtation, e.g. shopping center's facilities are enough or are placed to the suitable locations in order to let the shopping center's customers to feel comfortable to shopping when they enter this shopping center as well as whether the shopping center's facilities can influence the customer service staffs to serve whose shopping customers easily or difficult, due to whether the shopping center's facilities whether are adequate supplied or their locations are the best suitable positions to influence their service performance to let them to feel easier or comfortable to serve their customers in any large size shopping centers. For example, whether the lamps' lighting energy is enough to let the shoppers to feel safe to walk to visit any shops when there are many shoppers were walking to cause crowd and they feel difficult to walk to avoid any body contact to any one in busy time when the shopping center has no enough lights to let them to see anywhere in the shopping center's dark environment. Then it will influence customer service staffs to feel difficult to find any shopping center customers, e.g. when two shopping center customers are fighting in one location where is far away to the shopping customer service staffs and securities in the shopping center, because the shopping center is large and it has no enough light to let the customer service staffs and securities to find their frighting location to deal their fighting behavior and other shopping center's shoppers will feel very dangerous to walk their fighting location to avoid to close them. Then, it will has possible to cause death or hurt to any one of these two fighting shoppers ,even other shoppers' life. Because the shopping center's securities and customer service staffs who need to spend much time to find their fighting location, it will delay they can bring the policemen to their fighting location when they arrive this shopping center's destination in short time in order to solve their fighting behavior to influence all shoppers' life in this shopping center. Hence, the shopping center whether it has enough lamps number and the lamps' light whether is enough, these lighting facilities will influence any shopping center customer service staffs and securities who can spend less time to arrive any locations to deal any urgent matters.

For another situation in shopping center, if the shopping center has no enough paying telephone service facilities to supply shoppers to phone to anyone when they feel need to phone to any in the shopping center. Then, it will lead to some shoppers decide to find where the shopping center's reception's telephone to supply to them to phone call to anyone. If they are ten shoppers are waiting to use the shopping center's reception telephone to phone call to their friend or family within one minute. Thus, it will influence the reception customer service staffs feel difficult to arrange how to distribute the only one telephone to these ten shoppers to use to phone call their friend or family when they are queuing within their one minute waiting time in the shopping center's reception. If these ten shoppers can not use the reception telephone to phone call anyone. hen, they will feel dissatisfactory and complain to the reception service staffs politely. So, lacking enough facilities in the shopping center's any where, it will possible to influence their shopping centers' shoppers to feel all shopping center's service staff individual performance to be poor. It means that if the shopping center expects to improve customer satisfaction to its customer service staff's behavioral performance, it meets have enough facilities to be supplied in the shopping center to let its shoppers to feel it is one comfortable and safe shopping center. In conclusion, shopping center's facilities will have possible to influence shoppers' feeling to evaluate its customer service staffs to evaluate whether their service attitudes are good or poor indirectly.

● Can facility management improve productivity

The productivity means resources (input) is therefore the amount of products or services (output), which is produced by them. Hence, higher (improved) productivity means that more is produced with the same expectation of resource, i.e. at the same cost is terms of land materials, machine, time or labor. Alternatively, it means same amount is produced at less labor cost in term of land, material, machine, time for labor that is utilized. So, it brings this question: How can facility management improve productivity? I shall explain as these several aspects, it is possible to be improved productivity from (FM) successfully.

Improved productivity of farm land: If the farming land has better facility management to bring advantages by using better seed, better facilities of cultivation and most fertilizer. It is in the agricultural sense is increased (improved). So, facility management can bring benefits to any land resource to raise productivity in possible. It implies that the productivity of land used for better facility management of industrial purposes is said to have been increased if the output of products or service within that area of industrial land is increased output aim.

Improved productivity of material: If the factory has improved better equipment by facility management method to assist skillful workers to raise the manufacture cloth number, then the productivity of the cloth number is improved by (FM) method.

Improved productivity of labour: When the factory has good manufacturing equipment facilities to be supplied to improve methods of work to product more producing number per hour, then (FM) improved productivity of worker. Hence, in any workplaces, when organization has good facilities, it will influence employees to raise productivities in possible, because they need often to improved equipment facilities manufacture products to achieve higher production number aim.

● Can facility management raise bank employee
productivity

Bank workplace environment is busy, the bank counter service staffs need to contact many bank clients to help them to serve or withdraw money from bank's counters. Whether does the quality of environment in bank workplace will influence the determination level of employee's motivation, subsequent performance productivity in bank working environment. For example, if the bank's staffs need work under inconvenient conditions , it will bring low performance and face occupational health diseases causing high absenteeism and turnover.

In general, bank size is usually small, it will have many bank clients enter bank to contact counter staffs to need them to help them to save or withdraw money. So, it will bring air pollution the crowd queue in every bank counter challenge when the bank has many people are queue waiting in counters to queue. So, bank working condition problem relates to environmental and physical factors which will influence every bank counter staff individual working performance to serve bank clients satisfactory. However, bank staffs need to deal many documents concern every client personal data every day. So, they need to spend much time to use computer and painting machines. This is particularly true for these employees who spend most of the day operating a computer terminal in bank workplace. As more and more computers are being installed in workplaces, an increasing number of business has been adopting designs for bank offices installment. So, bank needs have effective facilities management design because of demand of bank staffs for more human comfort.

An good equipment facility management for bank staffs to use conveniently, it is assumed that better workplace environment can motives bank employees and produces better productivity. Hence, bank office environment can be described in terms of physical and behavioral components to influence bank staffs to work inefficiently. To achieve high level of bank employee productivity, bank organizations must ensure that the physical environment in conductive to bank different department organizational needs, facilitating interaction and privacy, formality and informality, functional and disciplinarily, e.g. house loan or private loan departments, counter service department, visa card application department.

Thus, in a high safe privacy facility management working environment will let different department bank staffs feel safe to worry about privacy loss in possible. So, the improving bank facility to bring safe and high privacy to avoid bank client individual loss in working environment issue, the facility management can be results to bring these benefits, such as in a reduction in a number of complaints and absenteeism and an increase in productivity.

● Can (FM) create value to organization?

(FM) can reduce managing facilities as a strategic resource to add value to the organization and its overall performance, e.g. saving the energy in building and take care of shuttle buses and parking facilities space management for , on economic efficiency and effectiveness, or good price and value for the organization.

If the organization expects to apply (FM) process to save energy, it depends on possible input factors, i.e. interventions in the accommodation facilities services. So, it seems that the organization expects to save its energy consumption in its building. It needs have good space management facilities between parking its shuttle buses in its property's car park.

Why does space facility management is important to influence efficiency and productivity. For one school's building example, when the school decides none of the two gymnasiums student sport entertainment centers to be built in order to reduce financial cost and higher benefits. Remarkably, the use of space with the school overall strategic goals , such as creating spaces that better can support the teaching, motivate students and teachers, attract more students and increase the utilisation of existing space to accommodate an increasing number of students.

If it hopes to make high quality teaching facilities on student's choice where to study. The school will need to choose to build either one comfortable and new design facility teaching accommodation or build two gymnasium sport entertainment centers in its limited land space either for students' learning or sport aim. Due to it feels new teaching accommodation can make more attractive to increase students numbers to choose it to study more than building two new gym sport centers to let them do sport in school.

Hence, space choice (FC) management strategy will be one important considerable issue, when the organization has limited land space resources to make choose to build any constructions in order to increase many clients number. Such as the school organization has limited storage land resource to let it to build either two gymnasium sport entertainment centers or one new teaching accommodation in order to attract many students to choose it to learn. Hence, it needs to gather data to make more accurate evaluation to decide how to apply its space facility to choose to build these both kinds of buildings in order to achieve the attractive student learning choice aim, so whether the two sport entertainment activity centers or one new teaching accommodation choice, it needs to gather information to decide whether the school ought to choose to build which kind of building in order to achieve the increase of student number aim, so space facility management will be this school's land shortage problem.

● The relationship between facility
management and consumer
behavior

How and why shop facility management can influence consumer individual shopping behavior? If it is possible, what shop facility management factors can influence their consumption decision when they enter the shop to plan to buy anything. I shall indicate some shop case studied to explain whether how and why every shop's facility management can influence consumer individual consumption desire when any one consumer enters any shops.

● Shop's low ceiling height location (FM) influence consumer behavior
Can the shop's ceiling height influence shoppers' shopping behavior? Can the shop's variation in ceiling height can influence how consumers process information to decide to make purchase decision in the shops, e.g. for this situation, when the consumer enters the shop, he/she feels the ceiling height is low and it has a lamp will contact his/her head in possible. So, he/she chooses to move far away from the low ceiling location in the shop. It is possible that shop's ceiling low height and the lamp locates at the ceiling low height position will influence many customers' choices to leave the low ceiling height and lamp location, then the shop's low ceiling height will have possible to influenced many customers to choose to find the another shop to buy the similar kind of products , due to the lamp locates in the low ceiling height, so this lamp and low ceiling height will be possible factor to influence any shoppers who won't choose to walk to this dangerous location in the shop. If the shop's all spaces are ceiling height and it has many lamps

are located at the low ceiling height spaces. Then, it will be serious to cause many shoppers do not want to spend too much time to choose any products in the shop because they feel dangerous to walk to the any low ceiling height lamps' locations in the shop.

Hence, hoe to design the different concept may be activated by the showroom ceiling if it were relatively high, as it tends to be in mall stores, versus low, as it is in most strip mall shops and outlet centers. Relatively high ceilings may bring safe shopping emotion to let any consumers to feel thoughts related to freedom, whereas lower ceilings may let consumers to feel dangerous to walk the locations in any shops. Hence it seems any shops ought not neglect whether their ceiling height is tall and the lamps ought avoid to locate in any low ceiling height locations in order to influence consumers number to be decreased.

● Can house facility management influence consumer individual purchase intention?

When one new property is built, whether the property consumers will consider how the new property is facility to influence their purchase intention to the property will the new property's (FM) influence buyers in real estate markets' preferences choice and living interest. Any new property's internal characteristics of the house unit itself , such as rooms available, when example, of external are location, accessibility to utilities services and facilities will have possible to influence the property buyer's final property purchase decision, so it seems that even the property price is cheap, it is not represent the property buyer will choose to buy the property, if he/she feels the property's facility management is poorer to compare other similar kinds of properties.

So, it can help real estate analysts better explain and predict the behavior of decision makers in real estate markets. Property consumers will search for property information, concerns the property's quality, price distinctiveness, ability, facility management, service of the property's external environment to decide whether the property is high value to choose to buy to compare other kinds of properties.

However, the external environmental forces, such as limited resources, e.g. time or financial will influence whose property consumption choice and living the property's satisfaction feeling (represent) a feedback from post-property purchase reflection used to inform subsequent decisions. The process of the property buyer's leaving experience will serve to influence the extent to which the property consumer how to consider future next time property purchases decision and new information methods. Hence, when one property consumer chooses to buy a house, it refers house features are house internal attributes , such as quality of building, the design as well as internal and external design, which are important factors for a property consumer when he/she needs to select and purchases one house.

The other (FM) factors which can influence the property consumers' needs, include living space as features, such as the size of kitchen, bathroom, bedroom, living bath and other rooms available in the house. The environment of housing area is also important factor, e.g. the condition of the hood, attractiveness of the area, quality of houses, type of houses, type of houses, density of housing, wooded area or free coverage, slope of the attractive views, open space, non-residential uses in the areas vacant sites, traffic noise, level of owner-occupation in , level of education in level of income in, security from crime, quality of schools, religious of , transportation , shopping center, sport entertainment can be supplied to close to the house area. All these human related issue of the property's location will also influence the property buyer's living location selection. Hence, above (FM) influence property consumer purchase behavior, it is based on the relationship behavior. The consumer's house purchase intention and house features, living space, environment and distance to recreation center, supermarket, library etc. public facilities variable (FM) factors.

In conclusion, the house internal space facility management and external environment facility management factors will influence property consumer individual house purchase intention.

● The effects of in-store shelf design facility management factor influences consumer behavior

Can every store retailer's shelf design influence supermarket and large retail stores shoppers' behaviors when they visit the stores? However, currently many stores tend to build on traditional and repetitive design for their store shelf layout, it brings results in outdated store layouts.

Another important store shelf layout design aspect, retailer should consider carefully is the allocation of products on shelves. So, it seems that efficient shelf space allocation management does not only minimize the economic threats of empty product shelves, it can also lead to higher consumer satisfaction, a better customer relationship.

Why does supermarket shelves design is important? Any retail tore will sell product category within a shelf. They can use the same nominal category

, e.g. crisps next to light crisps, same food product shelf. Anyway, a goal-based shelf display can contain several product, that determine a common consumer goal, e.g. fair trade. Hence, these two categorical product structuring methods are also described in terms of how to put product, or food on shelf benefit and attribute -based product categories.

These shelf design food or product storing method will have more influence consumers to choose to buy the supermarket or retail store food or products more easily , due to products, or food put on their shelf very convenient and systematic to attract consumers' shopping consideration to the supermarket or retail store.

● Music (FM) environment influence consumer consumption desire

Is it possible that shop music (FM) environment can raise consumer purchase desire? In one shop or supermarket, it can provide soft music (FM) equipment to let consumers can listen soft music or songs in the supermarket or retail shop when the are staying to spend more time shopping and whether soft music facility can be expected to raise customer individual value-added options to the music facility shop in the supermarket or retail shop.

Can the music facilities prolong consumers to stay in the store? It is possible that tempo soft music can influence consumers to stay longer time in restaurants and supermarkets and retail shops. It is possible that the different types of music (FM) in any supermarket, restaurant, retail shop owning music listening facility shopping environment. It will have possible to influence consumers to prolong staying in their shops. For example, one wine selling retail shop has classical music (FM) listening equipment to let consumers to listen when they enter the wine shop, it is possible to cause consumers to choose to buy more expensive wine products. Some researchers indicate when the wine shop owns classical music facility to let all consumers can list classical music when they walk in the wine ship, it can evoke the wine consumers to choose to buy purchasing higher prices wine products in the long term classical music listening environment. Otherwise, in a fitness sport center, musical fir and excite or popular music (FM) environment can attract fitness sport players' emotion to play and kind of fitness sport facility longer time. Also, in one supermarket, the soft music facilities listening environment can persuade or attract food consumers to spend more time in the mall consuming food or beverage also purchase other products more easily, due to they will listen soft music to be influenced to choose to prolong staying time in the supermarket. It seems that it has relationship between retail shop's music facility environment and consumer's emotion will be influenced by these different kinds of soft music or songs to raise consumption desire in the supermarket, if some consumers like to prolong to stay longer consuming time in the owning music facility environment's retail shop.

In fact, some researchers indicate the owning background music facility selling environment's ship , it can affect consumer decision making, memory, concentration consumption desire. So, classical , jazz soft music facility ought be installed in restaurants, retail shops, restaurants' environment. Otherwise, popular , exciting, noise, pop music facility ought be installed in fitness sport centers, theme park entertainment parks business places in order to influence fitness sport players or theme park entertainers to prolong playing or entertaining time to feel real sport or entertainment theme park playing machine facility's entertainment enjoyable feeling as well as attracting restaurant or supermarket or retail shop's consumers to prolong their staying time to make consumption decisions. Hence, it seems that music facility environment can raise consumers' consumption desire in possible.

● University bookstore atmospheric factors how to influence student's purchase book behavior?

Any university bookstore how to do international control and structuring of book internal environment to raise students' purchase book desires in university itself school's bookstore, it will be one popular question to any universities. Hence, whether the university bookstore internal (FM) factors include: lighting, music, colors, scents, temperature, layout and general cleanliness as well as university external factors include: the university bookstore shape/size, windows, university parking facility for students availability and location, which can play an influential role of the university bookstore image in order to influence the university itself students to choose to buy books from themselves bookstore or university outside bookstores.

Whether the university student needs to spend how long individual learning time and how much learning nervous to spend time to choose any kinds of book in the universiity bookstore or outside bookstores, this issue , he/she will consider. Because he/she does want to expect spend much time and nervous to choose to buy books in any bookstore. If the university's bookstore physical location and internal (FM) image can let its target student customers to feel it's all book products are stored in any attractive internal book shelves places, e.g. the cheapest and the most expensive different subjects of text books are stored in one system method to bring the positive image of value and quality in order to let university target student customers can find their books' choice location to spend less time to search any books to read in the unviersiity bookstore easily.

However, due to learning time is shortage to every university student of the university's book shelves can display all text books in the attractive right locations in the university bookstore as well as the university's bookstore ought has an adequate space to let university students to walk to anywhere and find any subjects of text books and compare their book sale prices in the bookstore's any shelves' locations easily when they walk to the subject of book shelf location, then they can make accurate decision either to buy the right kind of subject book or not buy it to read in the short time. They will feel their book choice purchase decision making process won't influence their learning time in themselves universiity. Then, the university students will be influenced by themselves university's bookstore's attractive external university facilities in the university's any teaching places and the university's bookstore internal attractive environment facility image which can influence the students to make final choices to buy their liking books to read from their university's itself bookstore. Hence, the university's bookstore internal and external building environment (FM) design factors will influence its students whether choose to buy from themselves bookstore or another outside general bookstore.

● How and why does retail atmospheric environment influence consumers behavior in retail shop?

Any shop's internal facility management design can influence atmospheric environment to influence consumer individual shopping desire, e.g. colour, lighting, music, crowding, design and layout factors, which internal shop (FM) environment can influence the first time shopping visiting client ' cognitive process how to feel the shop store image. Such as if the store's (FM) environment can bring enjoyable and fun and happy image to let them to feel shopping's enjoyment.

In conclusion, when consumers will like to stay longer time in the store. Due to the store's internal (FM) atmospheric environment can attract them to stay longer time in the store. Then, the customer's shopping value will raise and it can bring purchasing intention and shopping satisfaction. How can (FM) influence retail atmospheric physical (FM) environment ? Can (FM) bring indirect relationship to influence how the consumer individual causes positive or negative purchase intention when he/she has influence to prolong staying desire in the store, when the shop has good (FM) , it will bring long time to make consumption chance in the shop.

● Facility management influences
consumer satisfactory service
level

Can facility management (FM) quality influence consumer satisfactory service feeling? Any organization's facility management can improve the effectiveness of the maintenance organization. It can provide improved operational and maintenance functions to maintain the physical environment to support the overall mission. However, any organization will consider whether it improves its facilities, it will raise consumer satisfactory feeling when it provides the service to them, e.g. education service industry, when students need to often to attend any school's classrooms or lecture halls, computer rooms, libraries, all these facilities will be student's learning environment. If these school facilities can be maintenance to let students to feel comfortable to enjoy to study in their schools' any learning locations. Then, it has possible that to bring their enjoyable learning feeling in theirs schools.

● How school's facility management influences student's learning satisfactory feeling.
However, in education industry case, the school's facility management has those criteria can be used to measure effectiveness. Student individual response time between the student's request for computer use service in school computer rooms, library reading service in school library , classroom computer facilities and tables, chairs etc. furniture supplies service and the facility management supply number and available to useful time. If the student believes that the response time is too long when he/she feels need to use any school facilities, the actual number of seconds or minutes, he/she needs to wait how long time to queue to use his/her school's any facilities in library, classroom, computer room. So, the student's queue waiting time to use any his/her school's facilities, it can measure the school's facility management effectiveness.

● Scheduling of preventive maintenance activities.
It schedules of any maintenance activities are not arranged effectively to the school. Then, it will influence students' poor learning facility service to their school. For their situation, when the school's first floor has two men toilets are damaged. They are needed to be required. However, it is

one week period, the first floor 100 students can not use the first floor men toilets. Hence, in this week, all 100 students need to go to other floors toilets to often use. They will feel busy and time is not enough when they need to attend to any classrooms to listen the first floor classrooms teachers' lesson. If he/she arrives the first floor classroom too late, due to he/she needs to go to another floor male toilets to queue to use. Then, he/she will feel angry and worries about whose absent or late attending classroom behavior when the lesson's teacher has attended early in the first floor classroom , and he teacher will need him/her to explain why he/she will go to this classroom lately, if his/her explanation won't be accepted to attend to the first floor classroom too late in the week. So, arrangement maintenance schedule to any school's facilities issue is importnt to influence student's satisfactory feeling to the school. Also, lacking of preventive maintenance activities will bring results in unscheduled shutdown of critical equipment can have an unrecoverable impact on the school's good learning environment providing to student's mission.

In fact, however in any organizations, such as school, ship, office etc. organizations, achieving balance of effectiveness and efficient difficulties and takes time and effort on the part of management and staff. It is not enough to establish an optimal relationship between these two parts. It has another factor that organizations need to consider costs. In today's budget tightening environment, decreasing expenses requires accepting a lower level of efficiency and effectiveness. The goal is to determine the point at which decreasing efficiency and effectiveness is no longer acceptable before that point is reached.

It brings this question : How to apply facility management knowledge to rise efficiency and effectiveness in order to improve quality standard of service to satisfy consumers' needs in short time? Such as school's facilities service case. What factors can influence student's level of satisfaction with regards to higher educational facilities services? It seems that any school's facilities will influence its students how to satisfy its education service indirectly. Because they need often to go to school to learn. So, any school's facilities, e.g. classrooms, computer rooms, libraries, toilets, lecture halls, canteens, sport and entertainment centers, research laboratories, school car parks, student enquiry counters, all these places to the school's any students will attend. So, how raise schools' facilities improvement to satisfy students' learning needs in the school's any locations which will have help to influence it student individual satisfaction level to the school's service, instead of every teacher individual teaching performance service to the school's students.

For any service organizations , such as hotels, restaurant, financial institutions, retail stores and hospitals etc. The physical environment can influence how customers' evaluation of their service. Due to service has intangible nature, so customers will rely on evaluate service quality.

Any higher education institutions are education service providing organizations. They need have comfortable and enjoyable educational environment to be provided to the students to attend the school's any places in order to meet whose learning expectations and studying experience needs. So, the school's facility management will be one factor to influence student's learning satisfaction when they expect to attend the school's any locations or places to let them to feel the school's learning environment have good facility management feeling.

In fact, if the school has comfortable classrooms or lecture halls educational environment to let its students to feel, it will bring assistance to raise their learning satisfactory feeling. So, comfortable learning facility management environment is one kind of school's facility service characteristics, it includes intangibility, perishability, inseparability and variability. So, they are every student individual learning feeling when they are attending to the school's any learning locations. So, school's facility management service feeling will influence whether they expect to choose this school to study. If the school's facility management learning environment is more comfortable and teaching facilities are better to compare other schools' facilities. Then, it will have possible to attract many students to choose this school to study. Such as any educational organizations, instead of the teachers (lecturers and professors) whose educational level is influence students number. The university's building environment will influence students' learning feeling, when they attend in the university. The facilities include laboratories, lecture theatres an offices, but also residential accommodations, catering facilities, sports and recreations centers because university students need have university life feeling to let them to fell the university can give welfare services , e.g. medical services, career guidance, sport entertainment, residential accommodation etc. service, instead of educational learning service in classrooms and lecture theatres. Hence, university's diversification facilities services are needed to satisfy university students to choose it to study, instead of university teacher's educational performance. When one student can enroll the university to study from secondary education institution. The admitted student will usually consider two aspects to decide to choose the university to study. One aspect is the academic programs, of sequence of courses choices and the another aspect is the university's facilities whether they can satisfy their university life need, e.g. library, dorms, bookstore, food canteen , gym's sport entertainment, education technological facilities in the classrooms and lecture theatres to let the students to feel the university's teaching facilities are achieved his/her learning demand.

So, these two factors (teaching and learning and facilities) are linked to each other to influence student's total school learning experience and attitude towards a particular institution and this is termed as value chain in the student's learning process in the university. Hence, student individual evaluation variables will include teaching staff, teaching method, enrolment and facility enough supply actual service need.

However, the university's facilities, such as any residential accommodation, canteen, library , classroom, lecture theatre, sport gym, entertainment center will be their useful facilities need to satisfy their learning, entertainment and eating ,even living need in residential accommodation in the school's learning life experience every day. If one student chooses to live in the university residential accommodation . All of his/her learning and eating and living time and spending will be calculated to the university's any facilities to let him/her to feel it can provide enough facilities to let him/her to enjoy.

Hence, the facility management factor, such as overall campus environment, library, laboratory, classroom, lecturer theatre size and facility supply of on campus accommodation, welfare right service, parking areas, cafeteria , sport center etc. They will be every students facilities service needs from the university supplies choice. So, any university ought not neglect how to improve itself university's space area facilities to achieve satisfy their needs after they choose this university to study. Hence, any university's facility management will influence how the student's satisfactory learning service feeling when he/she chooses the university to study.

In conclusion, better facility management will attract more students to choose the university to study. Otherwise, worse facility management will not attract more students to choose to study the school. Hence, it seems that the school's facility management factor has relationship to influence student's satisfactory feeling, instead of teacher individual teaching performance factor to the school.

● Property facility management influences householder buying behavior

One new property's low price is attractive factor to influence property buyer individual preference choice. Does the new individual's facility management factor influence the property buyer's preference choice decision, if the property buyer feels its facility management is better than other similar properties, even it's price is higher than other properties. I shall indicate some cases to analyze this possibility as below:

Some properties' facility management service quality has possible to create true value for any property buyers when they consider the calculation ingredients to make decision whether to new property has higher value to choose to buy. The factors may include: price, natural environment, transportation tools convenient available, shopping centers supplies, the neighour quality, and the property's internal facility management etc. factors.

In fact, car or house purchase buyers, they have similar behaviors. It is that car's buyers will consider the car's machines whether they are safe to drive on roads, instead price, manufacture loyalty factors. It is possible that the car's machines quality factor will be preference to any car buyers when they make preference decisions to choose which brand its cars are the suitable. However, if the car's brand is famous and its appearance beautiful and price is cheap. But the car consumer feels its machine qualities are unsafe to let the driver to drive on road. Then, the car's poor machine quality factor will influence the car buyer's decisions to choose to buy this car. It can influence the car buyer individual car purchase decision.

The car buyer's behavior is similar to property buyer's behavior. Although, the new property price is cheap, good neigh ours are living near to the new property's location, shopping centers and transportation tools are available to near to this new property's area. But if the property buyers' feels its facility management is poor quality to compare other similar properties. Then, the poor quality of facility management factor will have possible to influence the property buyers whose final buying decision to choose to buy this new property. It brings this question: How and why can the facility management poor quality factor influence property consumers' preference choice?

In general, all property consumers won't know whether the new property's facility management is good or bad quality , they need to spend time to visit to the new property in order to observe whether its internal facility is satisfactory to his/her acceptable level. In simple, their purchase decision will regard to how to allocate household budget, how the household's economic resources are influenced, e.g. for travelling, visits to restaurants, comparing the different similar types of property product groups, e.g. apartments or houses or houses of a givn size data. For example, if one property's room(s) size is (re) small to compare other kind similar product type of room(s) size. Although the prior property's price is cheaper to compare to the later properties. But, if some property buyers hoped the property has large room(s) size, then the later larger room(s) size which will be possible to some property buyer's preference choice. Even, their property price is more expensive to compare the smaller room(s) size of properties. Thus, the property's room size which will be one major factor to influence property buyers' purchase decision. room's size had relationship to facility management issue. Moreover, if the room's quality and design is attractive, then it will bring more attractive to persuade some property buyers to choose to buy them to live in preference.

Hence, whether the new property is good durable product feeling which will influence householder's choice. If the householder feels the new property has long term durable life to avoid to spend much maintenance expense when they have been living in the new property for a long term period. They will believe it has better facility management, quality to let them to live longer time and the most importance is that they do not need to spend any maintenance expense , due to the property 's any internal facilities are damaged easily.

The external factors may include: culture, reference groups, family, social class and demography of lifestyle as well as internal factors may include: feelings, past property buying and living experience , property knowledge, motivation of the property buyer individual psychology. These both factors can influence any property buyer individual decision making process to do final house purchase behavior. However, internal factors, such as: property knowledge of facility management and property living experience, e.g. how to evaluate to choose to buy the property , due to the property buyer's past living experience for the past property's facilities whether its facilities can satisfy its property buyers' comfortable living needs. This internal factor will be more important to influence any property buyer's property purchase final decision. If he/she feels whose prior old property's facilities are satisfactory. Then, he/she will compare this new property and old property's facilities to decide whether this new property is value to buy.

So, the old property's facility will be the measurement standard to compare his/her next new property purchase choice. So, the property purchaser will compare these new and old property's property facilities product knowledge to similarities among property alternative which will influence his/her final decision to choose to buy the new property to live.

It seems that property low price factor must not guarantee to attractive many property buyers' choice. Otherwise, it is assumed that many property buyers like rent or buy to live the property for themselves for long term intention. There are less property buyers expect to sell the first property to earn profit intention. So, they will usually consider whether the property is long term durable product to avoid to pay maintenance expense when they had been living in the property in long term.

Some factors that taking consideration are proximity to the specific location, housing prices, developer's brand, the payment scheme, reference group, which are not the main factors to influence any property buyer individual choice. Because property buyer's need is that the property has good facilities to supply to them to live, e.g. good heater equipment can provide hot water to them to bath in winter or good air conditioners can provide cold temperature to let them to feel cool comfortable feeling in summer in their homes. Good electric tools facilities , when they have need to use electricity in safe environment at home, e.g. car park accessibility facility , level of security facility , surface area facility and housing types, bedroom, bathroom facilities, quality of housing manufacturing raw material, house design , house durable guarantee, speed of complaint responsiveness, specification accuracy, confirmation of building plan service, showing legal file property purchase process service, finance instalments process assistance, speed of responsiveness, officers' skills of presentation. All of above these concern property facility management issues will influence any property buyers' final choice to decide whether the property is value to buy. So, facility management will influence property purchaser individual final decision in possible.

● Hotel facilities influence hotel consumer choice

Travellers choose hotel to live. They will consider price, room comfortable feeling, hotel location , gum sport or entertainment service facility supplies , hotel room booking service etc. factors to decide whether the hotel can achieve every traveller individual minimum living need. However, whether hotel facilities factor will be the main factor to influence travellers' living needs. How and why do travellers consider hotel facilities whether are enough supply or facilities of quality to satisfy their demand to cause their living choice to the hotel final decision.

Usually, hotel's customers won't plan to live too long time, e.g. more than three months in the hotel. Because they are travelling aim. It will bring this question: Does hotel facilities quality consider to influence their hotel living choice if the traveller is short-term traveller to the country? However , some travellers who have effort to spend money to live high class hotels, even their journey is short trip. Hence it seems that short trip , hotel living reason can not influence the high class hotel travellers' living comfortable demand to the high class hotel room. Hence , the high class hotel room's facility management quality is also needed high performance. Even, when they need to eat breakfast, lunch , dinner in the high class hotel canteens or playing any sport equipment, or gum equipment or wathching movie in the hotel's small cinema room . They must need high class hotel can supply more entertainment, restaurant , sport facilities to satisfy their comfortable needs in the high class hotel. Moreover, they must consider safety issue when they are living in the high class hotel. So, thy must demand the hotel have enough five fright equipment in their rooms, or corridors and the stairs to let them can leave the dangerous locations to arrive the most safe locations immediately when the hotel has fire accident occurrence in any where . So, it ensures that the high class hotel's customers must ensure the high class hotel's facilities can satisfy their any one of above these needs before they decide to live this high class hotel.

In fact, high class hotel's room price must be more expensive to compare the low class hotel. So, it explains why high class hotel's consumers will need the hotel has safe and good quality of facilities to let them to feel it is one reasonable price, safe , good service and good facilities' high class hotel to live. Usually, when the traveller arrives the country to travel, the travelers chooses the hotel to live, it is whose first time visit in common. So, he/she ought consider that the hotel environment seems it is good or bad to let the traveller to select to live. If the hotel's facility environment is new and beauty and design colorful to let the first time travellers to feel. Then, it is possible that good facilities environment can influence the first time travellers to select to live, even the hotel's room price is more expensive to compare other similar hotels in the travelling living places. Hence, it explains why hotel facilities can influence traveller individual room booking choice. When he/she is the first time to visit the hotel to select whether to live or not.

● How and why facility management can influence workplace productivity to bring customer satisfaction

Facility management is one part of manufacturers or retailers as their productivity in workplace as their input and functionalistics within physical environment. In fact, facility management in workplace may include: site selection, property disposal, site acquisition, workplace space allocation, space inventory, space forecasting facility management, interior furniture change planning, interior furniture installation, moving maintenance, inventory, design evaluation, employment satisfaction evaluation plan, external maintenance and breakdown maintenance, preventive maintenance, landscape maintenance, energy space facility management, hazardous waste disposal, capital , operating furniture budgeting. So, it seems that one workplace considered whether the workplace's facility is enough to let employees to work in order to raise efficiency and improve productive performance more easily. Then, it will bring this question:

● How and why workplace facility management can influence consumer individual satisfaction?

Strategic FM delivery is essential for business survival. I shall explain why for delivery is important to influence customer satisfaction. In business process view point, an effective and meaningful service to their customer , i.e. the user. For logistic industry, the product's delivery time will influence when the product can be sent to the user's arrival destination. If the product is delayed to sent to the user's home or office or any location destination. The reason is because the logistic product sender has no efficient facility management (FM) arrangement in its warehouse . Then, its warehouse lacks efficient (FM), which will cause users to feel its delivery service is poor and they will complain its delivery service staffs. Then, they will find another delivery service company to replace its service. So, it explains that logistic industry's warehouse (FM) service arrangement can raise efficient time to send any products to their customers in order to let they feel satisfactory service. For example, Amazon online logistic company's warehouse has applied artificial intelligence robotic tools to assist warehouse workers to arrange the different kinds of products to deliver to the right shelves . Then, the warehouse robotics will follow their right product shelves locations to follow the right products to deliver to US domestic or overseas product buyers in the short time and it can avoid the wrong products to deliver to the wrong buyers' risk. Also, the (AI) delivery tools can raise time efficiency to assist Amazon warehouse workers to reduce their work load, and tried to work in large warehouse environment. Although, its warehouse's area is large, the (AI) tools facility can help them to deliver the different products to different shelves in the right locations , e.g. exact product number and the kinds of product to be delivered to the right country' client's shelf location in the warehouse. Also, it implies FM is very important to influence Amazon warehouse delivery efficiency and avoiding delivery wrong occurrence chance. For example, the shelf location belongs to US domestic customers, or the shelf location belongs to Japan customers, or the shelf location belongs to Hong Kong customers, or any other Asia or Western countries' different customers' locations. The warehouse's facility needs have different countries' shelves enough space to put and it also need enough space to let the (AI) tools, robotic delivery workers and human workers both to walk to different shelves locations easily and the different countries' shelves number needs to be calculated accurate. For example, it has how many client number will buy Amazon's the kind product per day. If it has above 5,000 to 10,000 China clients to buy the kind of product. Then, it will need to make judgement how many shelves are placed in the warehouse. So, it can avoid to lack enough shelves to put any different kinds of products to prepare to delivery to China clients in efficient time and it won't avoid to delay to deliver to their homes or offices or any locations in China.

Hence, such as Amazon logistic case, it explains why warehouse's space shelves number and area or locations facility management can influence workers or (AI) delivery tools how to move convenient and avoiding the delivery to the customer's wrong destination chance occurrence and shortening time to deliver products to its clients efficiently. Then, due to the delivering time is shorten and the wrong delivery destination's occurrence chance is also reduced , even it can avoid to deliver the product to wrong client's destination occurrence. Then, the logistic firm's clients will feel more satisfactory to its product sale delivery service and their complaints will be avoided. Hence, it explains effective warehouse (FM) space management service arrangement is essential to any logistic businesses nowadays.

● Facility management brings departmental benefits

Why do organizations need have facility management (FM) service? As above examples indicate that (FM) can improve workplace environment facilities, e.g. warehouse environment to let workers to raise efficiencies or improve performances, even it can influence consumers to raise satisfactory to it's services indirectly, also it can help organizations' equipment to be used long term to cause old and are needed to spend expenditure to maintenance or change new equipment in order to improve better quality . So , it can assist organizations to avoid to spend more expenditure for new equipment purchase or maintenance. All these issues will be facility management service's benefits to an organizations, which can concern raising customers' service satisfaction, raising efficiency or improving productive performance, raising productivity, reducing equipment or property maintenance or new alternation much of expenditure spending, office or warehouse or any workplace space planning arrangement .

However, every organization will need a facility manager or manage whose team effectively . When a facility manager begins to apply FM techniques to solve business problems. The case for FM is made. It is a simple matter of demonstrating a qualified return on the investment required. Every organization's success, FM operation of three key activities: they include: needing a proper understanding of the organization's needs, wants, drivers and goals and knowing when needs to review its changing circumstances, developing an effective facilities solution o support the organization's needs, wants , property drives and contribute to achieve its goals both short term and long term, achievement of reliable delivery of that solution in a managed, measured manner.

So, it bring one question: What are the influential factors to be followed the right direction to FM manager's strategic FM operational decision? The influencing factors may include: ownership, governance sector, complexity and perhaps of most significant, the size of the organization's property portfolio.

In fact, major occupiers feel FM service need, they are large corporate organizations and public service organizations. Their aims usually are to raise. The most marginal improvement in efficiency or effectiveness, these aims are the great significance. Major property occupiers will already have a facilities department or individuals performing the FM function with another department like property, finance or human resource, sale and marketing's facilities.

Usually these FM need occupiers who will encounter this problem: How can apply FM service systems and processes to be developed to improve reliable service delivery making use of the economies of scale, not suffering because of the size of the problem. This question will be facility manager individual concerning question: How to apply (FM) technique to solve the improvement reliable service delivery making use of the economics of scale problem for whose organization?

In reality much of external facilities management benefits to organizations, instead of raising efficiency, improving performance, raising productivity, reducing maintenance expenditure, e.g. energy saving, reducing natural resource waste, increasing local employment, improving supply chain management are all elements of the FM contribution to every organization's need. Hence are the work life balance argument and provision of an effective and safe working environment that supports why some organizations feel need (FM) service to support their organizational development.

Moreover, on cost benefit of space saving efficient view point, space service cost reduction is a key driver for all organizations and the medium, or large sized players will benefit directly from a well coordinated facilities strategy. For example, application FM technique to help warehouse or office space area to save 50% space vacancy to let employees can move easily or putting enough furniture or equipment or many stocks can be putted in warehouses . So, paying more rent expenditure to rent or purchasing another new warehouse or office to satisfy workers or employees' working environment to be better need. If the organization has effective (FM) technique, then it has enough space vacancy to supply to the increase stocks number to be putted inside in warehouse and it can let workers to move safety in available to let staffs to move easily and equipment have enough space to be stored in the limited warehouse space problem.

For greater space savings benefits will bring either long term renting or buying of increasing offices or warehouse number expenditure problem to any organizations, when the organizations' cost or renting or buying accommodation probably accounting for 60 to 70% of total occupancy cost . So a strategic program to release space or the prevent the acquisition of moves can be the most significant consideration to any facility manager, with between 40% and 60% of the workplaces are unoccupied in most offices or warehouses at any given moment in time.

Hence, how to apply (FM) technique to save space occupied areas for employment moving or stocks or equipment saving need in offices or warehouses. This issue will be any facility managers' seeking methods to solve problem. However, the important major advantage of facility management to organizations is that the application of management principle to keep the organization's property assets with the aim of maximizing their potentials. Thus, any organizations' facilities have become important, due to the property facilities' worth will increase if the organization's facility management technique can protect the organization's facilities have good performance. Then, the organization's maintenance expenditure will reduce and it won't need to spend expenditure to buy any new facilities to replace old facilities , due to they often damage factor when they are used old.

In conclusion, it explains why effective FM combines resources and activities can raise work environment improvement, which is essential to the raising employee performance aim. For hotel living service case example, this industry must need have good facility management service because hotels must need to fully equipped in term and facilities for effectiveness to satisfy hotel living clients' demand , hotels ought need good facilities asset management style lead to effectiveness in service delivery, there are benefit derivable from the adoption of facilities management from which other hotels can learn from for their effective operations. Hence, it explains why effective FM can bring benefits to hotels' properties to be more comfortable, beautiful appearances to attract many hotel customers to choose to live the hotel. Because hotel's building industrial kitchens, rooms facilities, equipment , halls of categories, restaurant facilities, gum sport entertainment centers' facilities, fans, elevators, lifts, electrical installation, escalators, baking equipment, recreational facilities, including golf courses which will be important factors to influence hotel clients' comfortable living feeling, if the hotel can keep its all facilities in the best living environment often. Then, it can raise chance to attract many hotel customers to choose it to live. So , hotel industry has absolute need to implement effective FM strategy to keep its properties more attractive to satisfy its clients' living needs.

Instead of hotel industry, logistic transportation industry also needs effective facilities management in warehouse, because of the logistic company's warehouse 's facilities are good, then it will assist to raise employee individual efficiency in the safe and system shelve stored facilities in workplace environment and improving performance.

Consequently, it will bring the shorten time to deliver any products to clients to avoide the delaying time delivery in order to let customers to feel more satisfactory to their services. In simple, it seems that some industries need have effective facilities management techniques to help them to bring long term customer satisfactory feeling, worker individual efficiency raising and performance improvement benefits. Hence, it seems facility management techniques' demand will be increased to some industries in popular in the future because it has help to raise employee individual efficiency , productive performance and client individual satisfactory level consequently.

Facility management how influences employee Psychology to raise productive efficiency

● How to impact of workplace
management on well-being and
productivity

In facility management strategy, design can lead promotion, the value of offices that are enriched, particularly including warehouses, shopping centers to raise their market value. Moreover, effective organizations, such as raising powering workers when giving the effective design of office space. I assume that a good design of an interior office workspace environment seems a psychological department to influence staff individual emotion to bring positive power in order to raising productive efficient influence, such as in a commercial city office. So, it brings this question: How workspace management strategy can impact on staff's working behaviors in office.

In fact, office tasks general include various forms of productivity, e.g. information processing, information management and any clerical tasks by computerization. Hence, office productivity concerns how to influence each office white color worker applies computers to work in office. The office space can impact on white color workers' performances in these several aspects: feeling of psychological comfort, organizational physical comfort and job satisfaction and productivity, efficiency. So, it seems that office workspace design strategy can influence white color workers' working behavior and attitude and performance indirectly.

The office space management includes: how to removal from the workspace of everything except the materials required to do the job at hand, how tight managerial control of the workspace, and how to implement standardization of managerial practice and workspace design. So, these key ideas will influence how each white color worker's efficiency and productivity in office working environment.

For this office space design situation, a large unseparated small space size's space design can accommodate more people and so brings itself to economies of scale. As a result, space occupancy can be centrally managed with minimal disruptive interference from office workers. Indeed, many businesses now adopt a clean and fresh air office working policy because they have more employees than they have spaces at which they can work. This desks are either taken on a first -come first -served basis. (hot desking) or can be booked in advance. So , when a company has many employees need to work in a small space working environment. It must concern how to let staffs to feel more comfortable in order to reduce high psychological pressure to work in this uncomfortable working environment. Hence, it explains why workspace design can impact on office workers' performance in some offices. All these issues are assumed that empowering workers to manage and have input into the design of their own workspace, then the effective office or any working places space management will enhance wellbeing to bring workers' positive emotions and improving productivity. I also assume the space working environment design have relationship of these depend variable factors to influence office worker individual productive efficiency. The variable factors may include psychological comfort, organizational comfortable, job satisfaction, physical comfort and productivity.

However, office furniture , facilities will influence office white color workers' performance ,e.g. the room size whether is big or small for manage office worker, a high backed, comfortable leather chair is needed for office staffs to sit down to let more comfortable, the door and most of the walls need glass, the office room environment needs have sea-grass rug beneath the desk covering the immediate working area, the office also needs have plants and pictures, mail boxes, telephone and computer facility is needed. When one staff needs to send email or phone call or send letters or deliver documents conveniently. These office elements are essential in order to increase physical well-being and feeling of satisfaction to white-color workers. Hence, geren office and office working space design management is needed in order to influence white color workers' productive efficiency in long term.

● Effective workspace design can influence communication to raise productivity

Office white-color workers often need communication between their managers, supervisors, and themselves. Office communication extends from the way that a user experiences a service. An effective office communication can bring these benefits; Providing positive influence on decision making by presenting a strong point of view and developing mutual understanding, delivering efficient decisions and solutions by providing accurate , timely and relevant information, enabling mutually benefit solutions, building health relationships by encouraging trust and understanding between the high level, middle level and low level staffs.

Effective office communication needs to clearly communicate its nature and purpose. Good communication ensures that all service staffs are sending out the same messages. Communication is also important for ensuring the service understands what users requires and why he/she talks about understanding users' needs and communication receiver can have effective communication skill to understand what he/she needs the another to do and the another knows he/she ought how to work by his/her task demand. Then, it will shorten much time. If the office has 100 staffs need to often communicate. However, if the office has good space management arrangement to let every staff can communicate easily and walks to anywhere to find the right staff to communicate conveniently. Then, they can spend less time to waste on communication issue. Then, their productive efficiency will be also influence to raise.

● Health and safe work environment influences productivity

Is a health and safe work environment can raise employees' work productive efficiencies indirectly? How and why it can influence employees' productive performance? Some occupations' working environments are easier to occur occupational accidents and diseases risks when the workers are working in the high health and safe risk's working environment. Hence, health and safety issues at these high life risk workplaces can be considered as a key to influence employees' overall performance. The idea that health and safety management program have positive impacts on productivity.

When one worker needs to work in this high risk of health and safe workplace. He/she will consider whether how his/her work behavior will bring suffer serious injuries for shorter or longer time from work related causes in possible. So, he/she will work carefully in order to avoid injuries occurrence chance. It is possible to influence whose work performance, low productive efficiency in order to avoid any occupational accident occurrences in the dangerous workplace.

If the employee feels danger when he/she needs to stay in the warehouses stable location to work often. Then his/her absenteeism day number will have increase, due to he/she feels that workplace accidents and occupational illnesses and can lead to permanent occupational disability, when he/she needs to attend the stable dangerous workplace to work in the warehouse. Hence, he/she will choose to apply holiday often in order to avoid injuries chance increasing when he/she needs to stay in the stable workplace location in the warehouse. It explains why companies increase need qualified, motivated and efficient workers who are able willing to contribute activity to technical and organizational innovations. So, healthy workers working in healthy working conditions are thus an important precondition for organization to work smoothly and productively. Hence, a health and safety workplace environment can bring these benefits to organizations as below:

It can prevent among workers of learning work, due to health problems caused by their working conditions, the protection of workers in their employment from risks resulting from factors adverse to health. The placing and maintenance of the worker in an occupational, environment adapted to his/her physiological and psychological, capabilities, mental , physical and social conditions of workplace and adequacy of health and safety measures are needed to any employees in order to bring positive impact not only on safety and health performance, but also productivity. However, identifying and quantifying these effects will difficult to be measured as well as the quality of a working environment has a strong influence on productive efficiency.

For one aviation air plane manufacturing factory, where workplace can environment will have high risk to occur occupational related accidents to cause employees' injuries. Hence, employees will be consider themselves safety when they need to work in high accident occurrence workplace. The bad consequence will influence such as absenteeism day number increases, leaving this kind of aviation air plane job of employees number increases, low productive efficiencies, due to there are many proficient experienced employees who choose leave this kind of high accident risk occupation.

Consequently, any high accident occurrence risk workplace environment , employers need have good safe and health strategy to let their employees have confidence to work in this kind of high risk accident occurrence workplace if they expect low productive efficiencies effect is caused by high accident occurrence risk workplace factor.

● Employee personal

empowerment factor influences
performance

Is empowerment one good method to raise employee himself/herself effort in order to improve productive efficiency in organizations. Empowerment often consists of support groups, e.g. management's effective leading or trainer's training, course educational opportunities. Employee self-management education may impact to improve himself/herself job performance, e.g. increased self-empowerment, self-management skills and job treatment satisfaction.

Only organization's empowerment strategy can lead every employee to through improvements in the employee individual decision making efficacy, improvement task performance behavior by reviewing whether what are the employee himself/herself errors when he/she encounters any job difficulties, after he/she reviewed his/her task error and his/her manager feels his/her performance can be improved. Then, it can enhance satisfaction with the employee and his/her manage relationship and better access and raising efficient performance in possible . Hence, empowerment can let every employee to discover whether what task related difficulties he/she faces or encounters every day. When his/her manager give ideas to let him/her to know how he/she ought review his/her task error in a supportive education working environment, it aims to let the low performance or low inefficient employees to increase confidence to continue work in the organization. So, the employee turnover number will decrease , if the inefficient employees can feel that they can attempt to solve their task-related difficulties successfully by themselves. So, empowerment can increase social support, leadership and advocacy development , it has resulted in greater employee individual performance psychological empowerment, autonomy and authority to let every employee to feel to achieve to improve themselves efficiencies more effectively in any organizations.

For hospital organizational efficiency measurement empowerment influence case, how empowerment can influence hospital's efficiency raising? Efficiency is one of the most important indicators of hospital performance evaluation. Why do some hospitals' efficiencies poor? It is possible that mis management of resources, lacking health plan packages, e.g. coverage of basic health insurance, poor quality of care service, more payment demand for out-of pocket payment , quality of primary healthcare , healthcare providers neglect to concern potentially about service efficiency issues.

In fact, low hospital efficiency is the major problem to influence patients number to choose the hospital's medical service, e.g. when the hospital often needs patients to queue to wait for doctor's care medical service. They need to wait on hour at least or more when the hospital has many patients are waiting for its medical service. Then, it will influence them to choose another hospital to replace it , if the hospital 's medical fee is cheaper and it does not need patients to spend long time to queue to wait its medical service. So, service efficiency is important to influence patients consumers' positive or negative feeling to choose the hospital's medical service. Even, the hospital's doctors are famous or they own many medical working experience, if patients often need long time to queue to wait its medical service . Then, it will cause its patients number to be reduced .

These are variable factors to influence the hospital's inefficiency. They may include old speed hospital information system and medical record documents based on inefficient input and output variables. Input variables may include the number of hospital admissions, the number of nurses and the number of available beds. The output variable may include average of length of stay and bed turnover interval inefficient paper document record in the patient record administrative department.

However, to evaluate the hospital efficiency indicators may include technical, scale and managerial efficiency the out-based data development analysis approach and the variable returns to scales assumption was used. Based on the out-input based approach (maximizing the factors of medical service production), to increase efficiency the organization should be increased outputs.

Hence, when the hospital has good efficient evaluation method to measure every staff's performance , e.g. ward administrative clerk, patient registration clerk etc. Then, it can base on an put-put based approach and assuming a variable return to scale, there is capacity to improve technical efficiency and managerial efficiency in these any hospital different administrative units without an increase in costs and use of same amount of resources in relation to technical efficiency and managerial efficiency and scale efficiency of hospital's administrative labour individual task.

In conclusion, factors, such as modification of managerial practices, use of modern technologies tailored to the cultural, political and formulation of clinical guidelines to standardize the medical processes in order to reduce medical errors and increase the empowerment of health care buyers (

insurance organizations), length of stay, management hospitals by specialist managers, administrative requirement, full time hospital physicians, limiting the authority of decision makers in relation to the recruitment of staff in accordance with the needs of the hospital and optimal allocation of beds, conducting economic evaluations and the type of hospitals ownership had an impact on the hospital efficiency significantly. By increasing the number of beds the hospitals efficiency decreases. Otherwise, optimizing the bed size can increase hospital efficiency.

However, the important factor to raise hospital overall staffs efficiencies empowerment is needed to let every hospital staff to review whether why and how himself/herself error is caused and he/she needs to review his/her errors to avoid to be caused from any negligence again in order to avoid patients' complaints again or reduce the patients' complaint number aims. So, empowerment of staff himself/herself error review factor is one major raising efficient good method.

● How organizational facility environment factor influences new and old employees long term performance

In psychological view ,in any organization's environments, they depend on the types of social and physical environment factors to influence employee personal behavior how to be caused. How and why does the employee select to do whose behavior? If the organization's physical and social environment is better, then it may influence its employees select to work hard. It is possible to bring productive efficient raising consequence.

In fact, when one new employee enters the new organization to work, he/she needs to learn how to adapt to cooperate with the organization's old employees to work together. So, it explains how and why organization's physical and social environment can influence the new employee individual motivation of behavior to work. In regarding new employee individual behavior by new employer's culture expectations as well as new employees need to adapt of actions that are likely to productive positive outcomes and generally discard those that bring unrewarding or puniishing outcomes by new employer's treatment.

However, anticipated material and organization environment co-operation outcomes between the new employee and the organization old employees' cooperation, which are not the only kind of incentives that influence the new employee behavior of the new employee actions were performed only on behalf of anticipated external rewards and punishment from the new employer. In actuality, the new employee concerns considerable self-direction in the face of the new employer's organization's old employees competing influences. However, when the new employee has adopted an intension and an action plan. When, he/she works in the new organization for a period, he/she can't simply not back and visit for the appropriate performances to appear.

The new employee's new job goal will be motivated by enlisting self-evaluative engagement in activities rather than directly. By making self-evaluation conditional on matching personal new job standards, the new employee will give direction to his/her new job pursuits and create self-inventions to sustain his/her efforts for new job goal attainment. The new employee will select to do new task behavior to give him/her self-satisfaction and a sense of pride and self worth for the new job chance.

Efficacy beliefs also play a key role in shaping the new employees' behavior to do their tasks by influencing the types of new organization's activities and working environments, the new employees choose to set into any factor that influences the employee's choice behavior can affect the direction of employee personal career development in the new organization. This is because the organizational working environment influences operating in the employee how to select working environments continue to work. Thus, by choosing and shaping the new organization's working environments, new employee can have a hand in what they expect.

In conclusion , when a new employee chooses the new organization to work. He/she must need to adapt the organization's new working environment. If he/she feels difficult to adapt or accept to the organization's new working environment, then he/she will be influenced to work inefficient or poor productive performance , due to he/she feels unhappy to work the new organization's working environment and the new organization's manager will dissatisfy his/her performance and complain or give verbal warning to dismiss him/her. Then, it will bring the poor consequence to let the organization's inefficient productive performance effect. If many new employees feel difficult to adapt to work in the new organization. Then, inefficient productive performance will be influenced to keep a long term. So, it implies that the organization will need to change its organizational culture in order to let many new employees can adapt and accept this new organizational culture to work happily if the organization expects new employees work to raise productive efficiency successfully.

● Raising efficient and effective
interview psychological methods

In human resource department, interviewing and selecting the most right applicants to do different kinds of positions, it is one part of HRM function. If the interviewer need to spend more time to interview to decide whom is the most right applicant to do the position in one day, e.g. 50 at least , even more applicants number as well as he/she can also make the more accurate personal selection decision to choose the most right applicant to do the position after the interview day. Then, the interviewing process needs to be avoided to spend more time to choose the most suitable applicant to do the position within the day. It is difficult to judge whether whom ought be the most right applicant to do the position, if there are more than 50 applicants , they are needed to be interview in the day. The consequence will bring HR department can spend extra time to do the interview task, but it can have enough staffs and time and resource to do other urgent or important task at the interview day. It will bring this question: How to apply psychological method to raise interviewer's efficiency to shorten to spend extra time to do interviewing tasks ? I shall explain some psychological methods to attempt to let interviewers have more confidence to select the most right applicant in short time as below:

1. Behavioral interview skill

The interviewer can apply the actual behavioral interview method to let the interviewee to answer how he/she deals the matters, he/she feels that it is the best decision in order to judge and analyze whether whom applicant is the most suitable to be selected, e.g. describing the situation, he/she needs or the task that he/she needs to accomplish. The situation may be from a previous job, any relevant event, describing the action he/she took and be sure to keep the focus on him/her , e.g. discussing a group project or effort in the team; explaining what results he/she achieved, what happen? How did the event and what dis the applicant accomplishes? What did the applicant learn?

In the behavioral-based interview. the interviewer can need the applicant to attempt to explain examples clearly in order to judge whose analytical skill whether he/she is the suitable applicant to do the position. The interviewer may ask the applicant to identify some examples from whose post experience where he/she demonstrated top behaviors and skills that employers typically seek. To judge whether his/her examples should be totally positive, such as accomplishments or meeting goals, the other half should be situations that started at negatively , but either ended positively or he/she made the best of the outcome.

This behavioral interview test aims to review whether the applicant's every example answer, he/she can provide an appropriate description of how he/she demonstrated the desired behaviors. In the behavioral interview, the interviewer can attempt to judge whether the applicant has good imagine effort to mind any relatively small set of examples to respond to a number of different behavioral questions to satisfy the right example are applied to the right situations in the limited interview time. Hence, behavioral interview can let the interviewer to make more accurate analysis to judge whether whom applicant(s) has (have) good analytical effort to solve any work-related situational problems in the most reasonable way or attitude in order to select whom is the most right applicant to do the position.

2. E-mail interviewing in qualitative research

E-mail interviewing is another good interview method to select right applicant to do the managerial level position. E-mail interviewing can be in many cases a viable alternative to face-to-face telephone interviewing. Internet-based qualitative research methods may include online personal interview and virtual focus groups. However, it brings two questions: What opportunities and challenges does online in depth interviewing present for collectively qualitative data? How can in depth e-mail interviews be conducted effectively?

The applicant targets may be the top-level manager, advertising executive , sales manager, human resource manager etc. management position applicants. They need to answer any complex or difficult interviewing question by email in the limited time, e.g. how to solve one case study problem , how to give recommendation to solve the situation problem. The interview participants may be recruited by tool/method of psychological test questions, the interview questions may be interview guide in a single e-mail and follow yp, length of email data collection period may be up to 10 weeks, the number of e-mail or follow up exchanges may be several number. The electronic formal and require little editing or formation before the applicants are processed for analysis all e-mail interviewing questions. So, they need to answer any managerial case study problem in limited time. It is one good managerial interview test method to evaluate whether whom applicant has the best analysis effort in order to the managerial position, because they need to find the best solutions to give recommendations to attempt to solve any situational problems in any un predictive case study problems. For example, when the applicant or a focus group of discussion applicants whom need to spend the maximum half hours to give recommendations to discuss to solve one complex or difficult case study problem either between the interviewer and the another interviewee applicant or between the group of five to ten interviewees (job applicants) themselves. Thus, after the interviewer sent the one case study question to let the applicants to know by every email channel. The interviewer needs to judger whether whom one applicant or one of the focus group applicants their recommendations are the most reasonable to solve the case study managerial situational problem within half hour to one hour. Then, the interviewer can make more accurate judgement to select whether whom has the best analytical effort to do the managerial position.

3. The effectiveness of motivational interviewing for young or older adult applicants selection process

How can apply case management skills to be effective to prepare any interview motivation? How to do the most effective and efficient to meet the objectives of the interview? Some interview techniques used may vary the based on the individuals involved in the interview. For an interview with the young age applicant more require a different approach than an interview with a senior adult applicant. The following are one pointers to assist with preparing for the interview as below:

Knowing the purpose of the interview and what needs to be accomplished . What is the expected outcome? Gathering all forms that need to be completed or signed having the interview and making list of questions that need to be asked, knowing the key facts and topics to be discussed, during the interview. Gathering factual information that may be helpful. Opening mind is needed in the whole interview process. Making an appointment for the interview and arranging sufficient time to set fully participate in the interview. Taking notes during the interview, let the participants know in general terms the reason notes are being made and how they will be used, opening ended questions invite the applicant to provide more information usually begin with other words who, what, where, how, asking one question at a time and keeping wording simple and specific, defining any terms that may be unfamiliar to the applicant , giving the interviewing participants in the interview an opportunity to ask their one questions or to clarify anything that was discussed, closing the interview with a review of the information discussed and facts gathered, reviewing any follow-up that is to be done by the case manager or others involved in the interview.

In an efficient and effective interview, the interviewer needs have good body and spoken word communication to the interviewee or the position applicant. Because a good communication can reduce waste time or avoid the extended longer interview time if the interviewer can make good communication to impact good message to let the applicant to understand what is the mean to his/her interview question. What he/she wants to know, the total impact of a message includes ,e.g. 7 % verbal (words), 38% vocal /volume, pitch, rhythm etc. and 55% body movements (mostly facial expression). The interviewer's body and verbal behavior can make more clear message to let the interviewee(job applicant) to understand what answers are he/she wants to know mostly. Hence, an efficient and effective interview can let the interviewer to control and manage the whole interview to evaluate whether whom the applicants' answers or feedbacks are more reasonable to be acceptable to be better to compare other applicants to apply the position more accurately.

● What is efficient achievement of technological inputs factor in construction industry

What is organizational efficient raising actual mean? I shall indicate construction industry case to explain technological factor is the major factor to assist construction organization to raise efficiency. For construction industry example, improved productivity could be attributed to advances in and increased usage of information technologies, increased competition, due to globalization and changes in workplace and organizational structures.

For construction efficiency, the construction process can reduce waste in coordinating labor and in managing, moving and installing materials, loss avoidance. It can achieve efficient aim. The construction productive efficient concept can be defined efficiency improvements as ways to cut waste and labor. So, one construction organizational efficient achievement means that it implemented through the capital facilities sector, these activities would significantly advance construction efficiency and improve the quality, timeliness, cost effectiveness of projects in construction processes.

On construction industry technological factor influence hand, it can influence that construction productivity how well, how quality, and at what cost buildings and infrastructure can be constructured, directly affects prices for homes and consumer products and the robustness of the national economy. Construction productivity will also affect the outcomes of national efforts to renew existing infrastructure systems; to build new infrastructure for power from renewable to renew existing infrastructure systems; to build new infrastructure for power from renewable resources to develop high-performance " green building" and to remain competitive in the global market. If the construction organization expected to achieve effficient aim. It ought consider how to change in building design, construction and renovation and in building materials and materials recycling, will be essential to the success of national efforts to minimize environmental impacts, reduce overall energy use, and reduce greenhouse gas emissions.

However, construction industry analysts differ on whether construction industry productivity is improved by efficiency outcome. They indicate construction efficiency needs to reduce 25-50 percent waste in coordinating labour and in managing, moving and installing materials. This is the most minimum standard efficient achievement level to any construction organizations.

What are the factors influence efficiency to any construction organizations? An efficient construction task process is made possible by a range of information technological tools and applications, including computer-aided design and drafting, three and four dimensional visualization and modeling programs, laser scanning, cost-estimating and scheduling tools and materials tracking. So, high technological tool will assist to raise efficient construction process to any construction organizations. It can help them to shorten time and avoid materials waste and control cost effective estimation for any construction projects.

Effective use of interoperate technologies requires effective team cooperative processes and effective planning up front and this it can help overcome obstacles to efficiency created by process fragmentation. Interoperable technologies can also help to improve the quality and speed of any construction project related decision making, integrate processes, managing supply chains, sequence work flows, improve data accuracy and reduce the time spent on data entry, reduce design and engineering conflicts and the subsequent need for rework, improve the life-cycle management of buildings and infrastructure.

All of these factors will influence whether the construction organization can implement efficiency in success. For example, interoperable techcholgies include legal issues, data-storage capacities and the need for " intelligent " search applications to sort quickly through thousands of data elements and make real-time information available for on-site decision making. How to improve job-site efficiency through more effective interfacing of people, processes, materials ,equipment, and information. The job site for a large construction project is a dynamic place, involving numerous contractors, subcontractors, trades people and labors, all of whom must require equipment, materials and supplies to complete their tasks. So, they need to know how to manage activities and demands to achieve the maximum efficiency from the limited available resources. Time, money, and resources will have possible to be wasted when projects are poorly managed, causing workers to have to wait around for tools and work crews are not on-site at appropriate time or when supplies and equipment are stored in complexity or difficulty, requiring that they can be moved multiple time (time waste).

How to improve job site safety and improve the quality of projects, significantly cut waste? The use of automated equipment, e.g. for excavation and earthmoving operations, pip installation, concrete placement, and information technologies, e.g. radio-frequency identification tags for tracking materials personal digital assistants for capturing field data. These high technological tool can help any construction projects to raise efficiency to process improvements and the provision for real -time information for improved management at the job site.

Moreover, on mannal research and development tools hand, instead of data technological tools hand, any construction organizations also need to consider how to take a variety of forms: How to test field on a job site? How to arrange lecture shows in efficient way, seminrs, training and conference, and scientific laboratories time, human resource available arrangement, spending expenditure budget to finish. Moreover, effective performance mearements are enablers of innovation and of corrective actions throughout a construction project's life cycle. They can help any construction companies or organizations understand how processes led to success or failure, improvements or inefficiencies and how to use that knowledge to improve construction products , processes and outcomes of active projects.

The nature of construction projects, the industry itself, any construction organizations ought consider the construction working environment how to influence construction workers' emotions. For example, when the construction site is high levels, of noise, dust and airborne particles, adverse weather conditions,and other factors that can cause injuries and thereby reduce efficiency and productivity. New types of equipment can make an active physically easier to perform, easier to control, move precise , and safer for construction workers. Similarly, changes in materials can reduce the weight of construction components, make them easier to handle, move and install. Manufacturing building components off-site providers need more control conditions and allow for improved quality and precision in the fabrication of the component, One study that examined the relationship between changes in material technology and construction productivity based on 100 construction a related tasks, the study found that labor productivity for the same activity increased by 30 % at least when higher materials were used and labour productivity also improved when construction activites were performed using materials that were easier to install or were pre-fabricated. So, it seems material heavy can influence construction worker individual productive efficiency in site, if the material is higher , then the construction worker's productivity will be influenced to improve (Goodrum et al. 2009).

Thus, the factors influence construction organization's efficiency. It focuses on whether the construction firm applies how advanced construction technologies to assist its construction workers to work as well as whether its construction environment can let workers to feel safe to avoid life danger or accident occurrence. When the workers do not worry about whose life safety as well as they can apply advanced construction technology to assist them to work. Then, their productive efficiencies ought need to be improved easily. Thus, facility management and advanced technology will be the main factor to raise construction workers' efficiencies.

Psychosocial and medical interventions for mental and physical health facility management strategy

The business case for implementation science is clear: As healthcare systems work under increasingly dynamic and resource-constrained conditions, evidence-based strategies are essential in order to ensure that research investments maximize healthcare value and improve public health. Implementation science plays a critical role in supporting these efforts. This case concerns how management scinece solves psychosocial and medical interventions for mental and physical health facilities management challenges.

Implementation science is "the scientific study of methods to promote the systematic uptake of research findings and other EBPs into routine practice, and, hence, to improve the quality and effectiveness of health services." Implementation science is distinct from, but shares characteristics with, both quality improvement and dissemination methods. Implementation studies can be either assess naturalistic variability or measure change in response to planned intervention. Implementation studies typically employ mixed quantitative-qualitative designs, identifying factors that impact uptake across multiple levels, including patient, provider, clinic, facility, organization, and often the broader community and policy environment. Accordingly, implementation science requires a solid grounding in theory and the involvement of trans-disciplinary research teams.

Facility management, or FM, is a broad discipline that includes a variety of industries, from food to technology, manufacturing to e-commerce and beyond. But, though the core of each business may be completely different from even its closest competition, successful facility management practices are easily interchangeable from enterprise to enterprise. As a matter of fact, it is one of the only job titles that can be found in, basically, any small to large organizations, including public entities, like schools and hospitals, to private buBut, reciprocal tendencies aside, facility management procedures and techniques must be highly-specialized for the business in which they are being used. Because the discipline covers complex specifics, including business continuity planning and even fire safety, it's key that your organization offers a holistic outlook on its facility management procedures.sinesses, like those that manage their inventory in warehouses. The discipline of facility management encompasses – and why poor management could easily lead to an organization's demise:

Safety – It's the facility management team's job to ensure the safety of all of the employees and customers occupying the property. This responsibility spans all possible environmental health and safety issues, particularly ones that concern the building and its equipment, specifically. Failure to do so can mean serious business in the form of fines, lost business, or even prosecution if it was deemed that the manager or business' negligence caused casualties or permanent environmental damage. Fire, for example, is usually right at the top of the radars of facility managers because it's a preventable tragedy that, when prepared for sufficiently, can save lives and valuable inventory. A thorough facility management team can protect its company best by guaranteeing that all parts of the facility are up-to-code, its employees are trained well, and all permits and certificates are completely valid. This function entails everything from safe and efficient lighting to flooring choices.

Security – In regards to importance, second to safety is facility security, yet another important piece of the puzzle in which the facility management team must answer to. Though larger companies or ones with particularly pricey inventory or equipment might make the wise choice to outsource its security needs in the form of a private firm, it's still the role of the facility manager to ensure that the firm performs competently. Technology advancements like biometrics and wearables are making it possible to maintain strict access control for high-security areas, but it's up to facility managers to stay on top of these developments and make smart security technology investments. In addition to general safety, it's also important that the facility management team has the technological know-how to safeguard and maintain its priciest hardware. This role is a key one as it doubly affirms that assets are protected just as closely as the safety of the community.

Maintenance and Inspections – No matter the focus of the organization, one of the most heedless things that a facility management team can do is slack off on its building maintenance duties. Every part of the building, including installed machinery such as HVAC systems, must be maintained by the facility management team. Because some facilities contain countless elements that need regular maintenance, establishing and following strict maintenance schedules helps to ensure that all moving and permanent parts of the facility stay up-to-date and working well into the future. Along with general maintenance, inspections are also something that facility management teams must always be ready for. They can prepare the business by conducting internal inspections, as needed, for the many formal regulatory inspections they might incur annually. Of course, the team must also take into account any time the facility undergoes a major change in hardware, level of inventory, or capacity – and, they must also keep their eyes on all changes in laws that could affect their current procedures.

Business Continuity Planning – Part of leading an effective facility management team means planning for "worst case scenarios." This means that each team must sit down with the powers that be to come up with a plan in case disaster strikes and the business can't afford to shut down operations. For example, let's say that a community college endures a major fire and the authorities have deemed the entire main building a total loss. The community college is currently in the middle of a semester which it can't cut short – this is a situation where prior business continuity planning is key. If this were done in the aforementioned scenario, the facility management team would have already come up with alternate locations to hold classes and operate the organization's administrative duties. In addition to the new venue, the team would have already made a solid plan for the temporary facility's security, maintenance, and hardware needs.

Daily Operational Duties – In addition to serving as the safety and security liaisons for the facility, it's also important that facility management teams are organized to handle the inherent day-to-day challenges that might arise. Depending on how the given organization is structured, this can mean anything from mending a leaky roof in the women's restroom to even fixing a jammed fax machine.

I shall discuss how to apply facilities management strategy to assist hospial organization how to raise its medical health care service to let patients to feel more comfortable and care for medical care in any hospitals as below:

Hospitals and health systems that engage in cost management are looking to reshape and reduce costs, and there are eight main strategies that can lead to effective cost management opportunities, cost management, at its core, involves two components: improving the planning and execution of current operations and attacking overhead costs and other costs that are "flying below the radar." Here are the eight strategies to reduce hosptial cost as below:

1. Understand the organization's readiness for cost management. Conducting a cost management assessment that details a hospital system's thinking, alignment, operational planning, overhead management and other moving parts could determine if a hospital is actually ready to begin a large cost management initiative.

2. Define cost-reduction goals based on the organization's capital shortfall. Revenue streams are not what they used to be for hospitals and health systems, and all cost-reduction goals should aim to close the capital shortfall as much as possible. "The goals quantify the performance levels necessary to fund the organization's strategies and maintain its competitive financial performance," according to the report.

3. Use internal and external benchmarks to identify possible sources of savings. Reviewing historical trends and applying global and departmental benchmarks and peer department comparisons can give a clearer picture of where possible savings could be.

4. Supplement benchmark data with other data analytics. Benchmarking data, while necessary and helpful, cannot map a cost management strategy alone. Using several data analyses, with input from medical staff and department managers, can hone in on cost-reduction opportunities.

5. Understand and focus on the key drivers of staffing and productivity problems. Inadequate plans, poor execution of staffing plans, unclear staffing roles, use of overtime and other staffing and productivity issues drive higher labor costs, which generally constitute more than half of a hospital or health system's operating expenses.

6. Drill down on staffing methods. Changing staffing methods could certainly keep costs in check, but it could also enhance the relationship between staff members and patient demand. For example, improved staffing in the operating room or emergency department will account for variations in patient volume but will still keep a strong semblance of patient contact.

7. Streamline overhead functions. Eliminating redundancies in human resources, accounting, revenue cycle, information technology, marketing, legal, materials management and other hospital functions can both improve operational flow and "yield large savings," according to the report.

8. Ensure cost-reduction targets are integrated with organizational plans and budgets. Inserting the cost management initiatives into the hospital's

strategic financial plan, annual budget and operating plan can allow management to monitor progress and report results to the entire organization.

However, above these cost management is accounting method to reduce cost in hospital organization human resource side, such as reducing staffs or staff number, reducing electricity fee. But, it does not represent the actual successful to implement the actual cost reducing, but it won't influence the patients' comfortable and enjoyable feeling. So, how to implement facility managment to bring actual cost reduce and avoid patients feel medical services are worse and lack of enough nurses or doctors number care need. I shall explain how to implement the new kind of facility management strategy to reduce cost and raise patients comfortable and care feeling in the same time to medical organizations as below:

● What is the new model of healthcare facility management

A growing number of healthcare organizations are moving to an integrated real estate model in an effort to better manage costs, respond to regulatory requirements, and support changes in patient care delivery. As healthcare organizations seek solutions to the challenges presented by today's evolving marketplace, it's clear that the cost and performance of their facilities will have a significant impact. Whether it's the need to drive cost reduction, respond to regulatory requirements or support changes in patient care delivery models, the effectiveness of an organization's facilities management program plays a critical role in their ability to provide high-quality, cost-effective patient care.

As healthcare leaders realize the importance of an effective real estate platform, many are finding that transformative changes are needed in order to realize outcomes that cannot be achieved under traditional facility management models.

● What is the tradition facilities management model to hospitals

Historically, facility management services have been provided on a campus by campus basis or separated into acute care and outpatient programs. In many cases, these programs have been limited to plant operations, which are segregated as an individual support service and function in a silo environment. Due primarily to organic growth or mergers and acquisitions, healthcare systems often find themselves managing their facilities in a bifurcated manner, with individual hospitals operating more or less autonomously. While many organizations have identified the goal of standardizing real estate operations across their system, it's common to find that these initiatives have been in the planning stage for some time. As a result, the inability to proactively manage facility costs and performance at the system level continues to be an obstacle to progress. Although facility management teams may have a "best-in-class" process at an individual hospital, a lack of resources or resistance to change may prevent that process from being consistently implemented across the system. As each individual campus makes incremental process improvements, they move further and further away from a comprehensive real estate solution. Recognizing that future success will require a systemwide approach to facilities management, continuing with the status quo model increases the cost of change in the future and forfeits the savings that can only be achieved through a centralized real estate platform.

The lack of a comprehensive real estate delivery model also inhibits an organization's ability to effectively develop essential programs at the system level. Services which are critical for long-term success, such as work order management, energy management, benchmarking, and standardization, are often pursued on a campus by campus basis. These initiatives require the dedication of significant time and resources to collect and reconcile data before creating and implementing the new program. So, successful facility management to any health care or hospital organizations. It must help them to bring cost reducing benefits.

With disparate facilities management systems at each campus, the process must then be repeated across the system. When evaluating the benefits to be gained through individual campus initiatives, consideration must be given to the cost of replicating the process as compared to the cost and time to market to create one process for the entire real estate portfolio. The lack of a consistent facilities management program also creates challenges related to business planning at the system level. A common example may be seen in the capital planning process, as the prioritization of projects breaks down due to a lack of reliable comparison data and the absence of analytics based on performance and cost projections. The process then becomes politically driven, rather than following a disciplined approach based on projected need and justified by consistent business case analyses.

A similar result is frequently displayed when organizations attempt to implement segregated processes related to space allocation to any hospitals or medical care organizations. The practice of assigning space based on availability is common, but it creates higher occupancy costs and difficulties in forecasting future demand and associated expenses. This reduces the accuracy of the business cases that drive the decision making process. Hence, one excellent facility management medical organization , it ought can reduce cost , but it can also let patients feel more large area occupancy patients rooms or any occupancy area to toilets, bath rooms , cooking rooms in any hospitals locations. It aims to let patients to feel comfortable and enjoy to live in the hospital. Without a comprehensive approach to facilities management, the space allocation process becomes reactive and can lead to the unnecessary construction of new space, when the reality may be that a solution is achievable within the organization's existing real estate.

● Approach to reducing costs

The challenges caused by the lack of a systemwide facility management platform are exacerbated by the traditional approach to reducing costs, which is to cut staffing levels. In the absence of a comprehensive facility management program, these staffing cuts are often a reactive response to an immediate need to reduce costs rather than a component of a long term plan. As the ability to focus on preventive maintenance decreases, the organization's risk increases and employee satisfaction and performance decreases. At some point, doing more with less is counterproductive and a new approach is needed. In order to achieve significant improvement, the status quo model must be transformed as part of a centralized delivery model to optimize the performance of facilities and create financially sustainable real estate practices. A comprehensive facility management plan will provide alternative paths to achieving cost reductions, as well as processes to ensure the continued support of patient care.

● The path to a solution

In order to achieve lasting results, healthcare organizations should embark on a process to consolidate their existing facility management services into a systemwide, best-in-class real estate platform. With the volume of changes impacting the healthcare market, having best-in-class facility management will be critical to long-term success. All aspects of facility services should be included as a baseline delivery model, with adjustments made in policies and processes to address different facility types. This system-based approach to planning and analytics provides a substantial competitive advantage. Given the time involved in developing and fully implementing real estate plans, organizations that pursue integrated facility management models will have an advantage over their competitors who continue operating as they have in the past.

A systemwide real estate program, including facility management, project management, facility activation services, property management, strategic real estate planning, real estate accounting and market-based transaction management allows organizations to successfully implement proactive initiatives such as ambulatory prototyping, site selection, labor analytics and workplace environment optimization. Once the assessment is complete, it will be possible to produce a gap analysis to identify opportunities to reduce costs and improve processes and performance. These opportunities can then be evaluated by weighing the cost to implement new system based programs against the expected savings or operational benefits. Each opportunity should be validated as part of a consistent decision process, allowing prioritization based on an organization's overall business plan and appetite for change.

Once the facility management program is on its way to best-in-class status, it should be integrated with all other real estate services to fully optimize performance. Ideally, this transformational process will follow concurrent and coordinated schedules across all real estate services, with the objective of developing supportive and complimentary processes among all teams. As the delivery of patient care evolves, the delivery of real estate services must transform to keep pace. The solution is to transition to an integrated systemwide real estate model, drawing on examples of successful platforms and driving improvements based on quantifiable data and objectives.

As part of an integrated platform, these programs allow organizations to fundamentally change the way real estate is managed, dramatically reducing year over year expenses and enabling the accurate prediction of future space requirements and the reliable forecasting of associated long term financial obligations. When truly integrated, the real estate platform will provide cost-effective management of assets and contribute significant value to many internal departments, including strategy and business development, clinic systems, finance, compliance, and procurement. The benefits of an integrated real estate platform cannot be achieved without completing a comprehensive transformation of the traditional model.

On conclusion, in order to achieve that goal, healthcare organizations should pursue the transformation of their real estate platform by taking the first steps towards a best-in-class facility management program. Successful healthcare organizations of the future will have integrated real estate services, with facilities that operate at peak efficiency and are proactively managed to respond to and support changes in the delivery of patient care.

Reference

Becker, F. (1990). " Facility management : a cutting edge field?" property management 8 (2): 25-28.

Bernard, M.B. & Bruce, J. A. (1994) Improving organizational effectiveness through transformational leadership: US. Sage publications, Inc. pp. 11-13.

Fiona, M.W. (2004). organizational behavior and work , a critical introduction, 2 ed. : New York, US, Oxford university press, pp.79 .

Jac, F.E.& John , R.M. (2014) predictive analytics for HRM:US Pearson Education pp.13-16

Stephen, P.R. & Timothy, A.J. (2018). Essentials of organizational behavior, 14 ed.: US. Pearson Education, Inc. pp.108-110.

FM and technology how improve organizational efficiency

Human Behavioral network job brings social economic benefits

What does human network job mean ? Why may human network job be popular? Why human network job behavior may influence economy ? Nowadays internet is popular to use. We can apply internet to find data , search any new things, even earn money. Why does internet

may become huma network job source. For example, e-publish may be one kind of new human network job. Any authors may apply internet

channel to help them to sell electronic or paper books from e-publisher web store. They may apply facebook, you tub etc. any online

channel to promote themselves new books to let new readers to know whether when they may buy themselves favourable new topic books to read from electronic publisher web store.

Thus, future electronic publisher industry may help any authors to build internet network platform to help them to sell and promote

ot advertise their any one new electronic or paper book topic to let global any one reader to choose to buy their any new topic books from electronic publisher web store easily and conveniently. However, it implies that electronic network platform author may be one kind of future new human network job in our societies.

How electronic network platform author job may bring economy benefit in macro economy view? A person can have few friends, contacts and still be very influential if these few

friends and contacts are themselves highly influential, e.g. one author must not need to know any one reader in global society. When they like to choose any electronic books from electronic internet network platform. They may become the author's any one topic book buyer, when they feel the author's any one topic book is fun and attract they make decision to buth the strange author whose the topic book from electronic book publisher's platform web store conventiently in short time. Although, they are strangers, they do not know themselves , but the reader can understand what it way that made Google from writing platofrm to create new creative mind and typing network job method to replace traditional hand writing book method for global authors. It will be one kind of new human network writing job.

Hence, global any one reader can apply an innovative search engine , such as google.com to find whether whom author personal new topic books are value to read from internet.

Then, the electroniuc publisher's web store may be new book store platform sale network to help the author to sell many electronic or papcr books from electronic network platform

in short time. So, internet may be future new network plaform to help global any one author to create network writing job absolutely. Furthermore, internet may be popular social media

to help any one author to build goold relationship between his/her readers. It is one kind of new network, human network job. New authors do not need to buy many paper books to prepare to put in any one book shop warehouse. Their every book can print on demand to reduce out of book stock in any one book shop. They may choose to sell either electronic books or paper books both from any one book publisher web store. So, electronic network platform may be one kind of good writing channel to help human authors to create income and it can also help authors to bring new creative mind and new topic fun content books to let readers to know and buy to read from electronic publisher network platform.

Why does human behavior may be one kind of new human network job to bring global economic advantages. ALthough, it may be free income or without inocme, but the person does the network behavior, his/her behavior may be bring advantages to influence many other people's health. For this case, when a worker in a coffee shop in an airport gets a vaccination againinst the flu, it does not only helps him or her stay healthy, but also helps the many travellers who might otherwise have been inflected if that workers caught the flu. So, the externality , the result implies the vaccination of even a part of a community conveys benefits to the whole community. For example, governments pay special attention to the vaccinations of school children, teachers, health mothers, and the elderly, categories of people particularly susceptible not only to catching, but also to transmitting a disease.

It is not accidental that governments are heavily involved with vaccination . When there are externalities, free market, fail to persuade individual incentives with society's

their the worker's decision of whether to get a vaccine ends up attracting whether other people get sick. The workers might not fully take all these other people's potential suffering into account when making her or his vaccination decision.

As Stanford University does many suggestions, understand this and tries to help them make the right decisions and so providers free flu vaccines for its staff and students.

Small pockets of unvaccinated individuals can allow a disease to gain a spread more widely well-being. For example, parent weighing the costs and benefits of a vaccine for their child is not always thinking of the consequences of that vaccination to other people. THese are markets in which subsidizing or regulating behavior can make everyone better off. Because the reason for requiring that a child be vaccinated before enrolling in school is not just to protect that child, because each child's vaccination affects others via potential contagions.

Robots take our jobs behavioral and economy influences

Robot job behavior brings economy influences

If one day robots can replace human to do simple, even complex jobs. They will bring what influences to our global societial economy.The popular economic refrain declares that the

global middle class is dying and robots will soon take our jobs, e.g. shopping center customer service jobs, library service jobs, cinema ticket sale jobs, restaurant kitchen cooker jobs,

even, bus drivers, taxi drivers etc. public transport driving jobs, accountant, doctors etc. professional jobs. Whether it is beautiful or petty matter if our future societies have many human jobs can be replaced to do from robots. Businessman must may reduce to employ employees and reduce to pay salary or wage, when robots can be replaced to do their employees tasks. But, societies must bring unemployement rate rises , due to societies will have many people loss jobs when their employers choose to buy robots to serve their clients or do any office tasks or customer service or cleaning etc. tasks.

In micro economy view, employers may save money in long term, but in macro economy view, it will cause unemployment ratio rises , even crime rate rises when there are many people lose

jobs in societies. These models of doom, though, fail to account for the hundreds of businesses riding the waves of change in their industries when robots may be invented to replace human to do many simple , even complex tasks in our future societies.

WE may image that one small factory needs to manufacture fishes canes to sell to supermarket, the small , cheaper stuff and higher margin parts of the fishes manufacture industry. Before, this factory needs to employe many human factory workers need to help every fresh customer makeing the perfect fishing gear, designed for performance, durability, and cost in order to achieve to manufacture every fish cane in whole fished processing manufacturing stages. Every worker needs to spend about 15 to twenty minutes to finish every fish cane , till to delivery to any supermarket to sell. If this fish canes manufacturing factory can apply manufacturing robots to help them to finish any one working tasks , every robot can only spend five minutes to finish whole fresh fish cane manufacturing process. Thus, every robot can

help this factory save 10 to 15 minutes time to finsh every fish cane manufacturing process. IN fact, time is money, because when every robot can help this factory to reduce 10 to 15 minutes time to compare human worker. Then, this factory can finish about 20 fish canes in one hour if it can use robot to help it to manufacture fish canes. Otherwise, if this factory still use human workers to help it to manufacture fish canes, then it can finsh about 3 to 4 fish canes in one hour. SO, the manufacturing efficiency ensures that robots must help this fish manufacturing factory to raise fish canes number more than human workers. So, in robotic behavioral economy view, manufacturing robots must help this fish canes manufacturing factory to raise fish canes manufacturing number and deliver increasing number to supermarkets to prepare to sell every day. Robots can help this fish canes manufacturing factory bring manufacturing time saving, rising manufacturing efficiency, improving performance and reducing wages expenditure long time advantages in micro economy view. However, manufacturing robots can also bring disadvanages to society, e.g. increasing unemployment ratio, increasing crime rate,

this factory workers will lose jobs and income, they need earn social welfare from government and increasing government finance pressure in short time, even long time in macro economic view.

Stanford University graduate program in economics, Scott lecturer explained that "in demand and supply economic theory for robots supply and demand case, robots supply number increasing may influence human workers demand number decrease. It sometimes calls " the efficient frontier".

No specific human beings were mentioned in any of economics classes. As robots supply and demand in market case, They (robots) may be purely theoretical " agents" who reached to the most reasonable sale prices in order to persuade any one businessman buyer to make manufacturing robot buying decision whether robots can help him / her to bring how much saving time , saving money, saving cost, improving performance, efficiency economic benefit before he/she plans to reduce workers number when he/she decides to apply robots to replace human workers in his/her factory or office or any service department, e.g. cinema ticket sale service, shopping center customer service, shopping center cleaning , supermarket customer service etc. service or sale tasks. When robots can replace human to do any one of these tasks in any organizations. So, robots may be human worker agents who reached to prices the way robots would react to a software command. There was nothing that explained why some people thrived and others did n't or why truly brilliant, hardworking people could fail when much lazier folks succeeded." Having been admitted to the Stanford University graduate program in economics, Scott lecturer hoped to get his answers there.

How robots influence our future social changing? Using the right technology can be a boon to your business in this economy. For internet example, it is easier than ever to find well-matched customers all around the world, to stay in contact with them, and to more quickly design the products they want. If you focus solely on being cutting -edge, though you risk letting the technology
take over what should be very robust relationships with your customers , employees, and colleagues. IN nowaddays society, technoligical advances and cutomation, personal
relationships in business are more crucial than ever. I mean that robots can not replace human to serve clients to let them to feel more comfortable and passion more easily. For shoe shop case example, if the shoe shop apply one robot to serve its clients to replace human shoe salesperson to serve its shoe customers. Robots ensure that they can not persuade every shoe potential buyer to make shoe buying decision more easily when robots need to contact every shoe potential buyer. The reason is simple, because robots can not touch any one shoe buyer individual emotion very easier.

If the shoe buyer needs the robots to help him/her to choose any right shoe styles when he/she can not feel himself / herself can make the most right shoe style choice decision. The robots can not replace human shoe salesperson to make shoe style choice judgement more easily. They must need longer time to analyze whether which shoe style may be the most suitable to the shoe buyer. Otherwise, human shoe salesperson may attempt to make the most right shoe style choice decision to help any one shoe buyer to chooce the most right style shoe because he/she owns shoe style sale experience, shoe style knowledge, the most important reason is that they can feel every shoe customer individual emotion to touch whether he/she will feel comfortable or happy when they attempt to help every shoe customer to seek the most right shoe style in every shoe customer whole shoe searching processing. Othwerwise, serving robots are only one machine, they can not touch or feel every shoe customer individual emotion whether he/she feel comfortable or unhappy or happy when they need to contact them in whole shoe searching processing. Hence, I believe that some tasks robots can

not repalce human staff to do very easily. Otherwise, robots may bring disadvanatges to let any one businessman to loss his/her customers, due to robots can not touch every customer

emotion to compare human staff in service tasks more easily. Robots serving customer behaviors may cause money lose and customers number lose to the shop in micro economic view.

Intellectual human economic behaviors

What does intellectual human economic behaviors mean ? I believe that when we choose or decide to do intellectual behaviors, then our societies will be influenced to bring economic growth in consequence.I shall attempt to indicate pollution case to explain how and why eithet our intellectual or foolish behaviors may bring economic growth or recession in consequence as below:

On one hand, for air pollution social case aspect example, if we only consider to buy cars to drive for working aimr or holiday leisure aim. Then, our societies air will be polluted. Our health will be influenced to bad. Our car driving behaviors may cause global environment air pollution serously. In long tiem, global air pollution will bring our bodies health to be bad. Although, ourselves car driving behaviors may bring our driving travelling leisure enjoyment and comfortable feeling in short time, also we so not need to pay public transport fare often, but we need to compensate ourselves health economic intangible loss due to air pollution , when cars number increases, dirty air will cause ouselves health to become bad.

In the result, we will need to pay more medical expenditure when we are old age, due to ourselves bodies will become bad, due to we breathe global dirty air every day, due to ourselves cars pollute air in long time, e.g. 10 to 20 years, even 30 more without limited air pollution environment. So, driving cars behavior may be one kind of human foolish behavior and our foolish behavior may bring ourselves future long time medical expenditure absolutely.

One the other hand, water pollution social aspect, if we often keep much rubblish to pollute sea, oil exploration porcessing pollute ocean , ships gas pollute ocaen, then fishes will eat polluted food and drive dirty water, due to global ocean is polluted.

In fact, because human only to conside how to buy boats to carry on leisure enjoyment activities, or catch cruises to travel on the sea. Also, oil manufacturers only consider researching anywhere to find new oil exploration places to manufacture oil product, when their oil exploration processes pollute ocarn . Consequently, global fishes drink polluted warer or eat polluted food. They will have poison. SO, human will have high chance to eat poison polluted fishes, due to fishes are poison or are polluted. So, human is doing foolish activities, we only hope to find oil exploration places to pollute ocean or we only spend money to buy ticket to catch ships to travel anywhere in global ocean. All of these human foolish behaviors will bring pollution to global ocean. On consequently, we will need to compensate to eat polluted or dirty or poision fishes, ourselves bodies health will be bad. In long time, we need have high chance to pay medical expenditure when we are old. So, pollution case may be one good example to explain how and why human foolish behavior may influence ourselves future need to compensate serious medical loss.

All of these human foolish behavior will bring pollution to global ocean. On consequently, we will need to compensate to eat polluted or dirty or poison fished , ourselves bodies health will be bad. In long time, we will have high chance to pay medical expenditure, when we are old. So, pollution case may be one good example to explain how and why human ourselves intellectual or foolish behaviors may influence future long time economic loss or economic growth or recession in micro and micro economic view.

On another water pollution aspect hand, if we often keep rubbish to sea, oil exploration processing pollutes ocean and ships‘ gas pollute ocean, then fishes will eat polluted food and drink dirty water, due to fishes will eat polluted food and drink dirty sea water because the global ocean is polluted seriously.

In fact, because human only consider how to buy boats to carry on any leisure water activities, or catches cruises to travel on the sea. Also, oil manufacturers only consider any where to find oil exploratin places to manufacture oil products from ocean, when their pol exploration processes can plooute ocean. Consequently, global fishes drink polluted water or eat direty food. They will have poison. So, human will have high chance to eat poison fishes.

Otherwise, such as pollutin case, it can infuence inflation or deflation. Consequently, the reason indicates supply and demand theory. If air pollution is serious, then we will consider health issue, global cars demand number may be influenced to reduce, when global cars number demand will reduce, global car prices and supply number will need to change to fall down in order to attract or persuade global car consumers choose to make car purchase decision.

Hence, global car manufacture number and car price will be influenced to reduce, due to global air pollution issue. Consequently, deflation will occur because when the country citizen usually does not spend much extra saving money to buy car expensive goods. Money value will be low. Otherwise, if global cair pollution is not serious, human considers to buy cars to enjoy driving leisure lives. So, global car demand is influenced to increase , also global car price will also influenced to increase.

Consequently, gobal human will choose to buy cars to drive. Due to we accept to spend extra saving to buy expensive car goods. Car sale price and supply may be influenced to rise up. Money value is influenced to reduce. Inflation may be influenced, due to global car consumers number increases, we would not have extra money to spend easily. Car expensive goods expenditure influences our spending habit to avoid to make car purchase decision more easily. So, human intellectual or foolish activities may bring inflation or deflation consequency in possible indirectly in macro economic view.

On conclusion, above pollution case explain that how and why human intellectual or foolish economic behaviors may bring inflation or deflation consequency as wll as economic growth or recession consequency as well as any goods demand and supply increasing or decreasing consequency. It implies that human behavior may have indirect relationship to influence any goods demand and supply number to either increase or decrease result as well as any goods price will be influenced to increase or decrease in micro and macro economic view.

The relationship between social change and human behavior

Why does economic changes may influence human individual behavioral change? I shall attempt to indicate shopping behavior and staying at home behavior to explain their case and effect relationsip as below:

Human behavior can be influenced by economic change or economic change can be influenced by human behavior? Why does recession may influence consumers reduce shopping desire? In social recession suitation, it is possible that many people lose jobs suddenly, due to businessmen lose many customers. They need to make decision to reduce employees number in order to continue to keep businesses. Consequently, many firms (organizations) their employees may lose jobs. When they have much time, due to lose jobs, they will feel to avoid to spend too much time and money to go to shopping often. Many losing jobs people, they will often stay at homes. So, they will reduce time to go to shopping, then non essential products won't their preferable choice purchase products. Hence, recession will change many losing jobs people their shopping or consumption desires to avoid to buy non essential products often . Usually when economic boom, many people have jobs to do because consumers number must increase when many people have jobs to do. Then, many people can accept to spend money to buy non essential products often. Many people feel spend time to go to shopping can satisfy their purchase of any kinds of new products useful psychology or desire. So, recession is one good example to explain it can influence many people do not like often to leave homes to go to shopping easily. Many people like to stay at homes, becaue they feel worry about spending too much shopping time when they leave homes. Their staying home time is one good negative shopping behavior example. So, economic change may influence human individual behavior changes , they have direct cause and efect relationship in behavioral economic view.

May human behavior influence economic change? Is it possible that human behavior may bring the country social economic change in macro economic or micro behavioral economic view ? I shall indicate publishing industry example. Do you feel that if there are many students feel learning is very important when they read many books or many of students feel interesting to read or they have reading new books in habit, then it is possible that the country will have many students like to spend time to go to any book shops to choose the books, they feel that they can help they learn new knowledge.

Then the country will increase students number, they often spend time to visit any one book shop every week. Their visiting book shops behavior which may become their habits. So, the country will increase students number, they often spend time to visit book shops. Also, it implies that visiting book shops behaviors may be their behavioral habits.

So, when the country has many students often spend time to visit book shops , their visiting book shops behaviors may help any one book shop to raise books sale chance. So, the country's student individual often visiting book shop behaviors, their habitual visiting book shops behaviors must may assist help any one book shop to increase books sale number absolutely.

Consequently, any one book shop , its books sale bumber must be influenced to increase to increase because the country will have many students like or feel need visit book shops habit in order to choose any suitable books to buy to read at home in order to raise themselves learning effort. When the country has many bok shops often have many students visit their book shops, then their books sale number may be influenced to increase. It explain why student individual visiting book shop behavior may help any one book shop sale number increases also.

How human productive behavior may influence economic development

May any country which citizen behavior assist themselves country development? It is one cause and effect economic question. I mean that if the country itself citicen can not concentrate mind or energy to choose to do one kind of industry in order to let themselves country can bring the most benefit, then whether the counry itself economy can bring the most serious economic benefit. I shall attempt to indicate these countries themselves indistry choice to explain whether these countries themselves citizen productive behavior may help themselves countries to achieve the largest economic benefits. I shall indicate as below:

New Zealand farmer individual wine productive behavior

For New Zealand country example, this country concerns itself effort is foucs on farming agricultural aspect. So, this country has many farmers concentrate on farming agricultural aspect. May New Zealanders choose to spend time to produce different kinds of wines, e.g. wine or red grape wine is for the people are eating meat, or they are eating dinner.

When these New Zealanders their behaviors choose to do farming or agriculture to grow and produce different kinds of taste of white or red grape wine drinking products job. Themselves grape agriculture behavior will influence these New Zealanders themselves, they can learn how to improve different kinds of grape wine drinking products in order to achieve every kinds of white or read grape wines taste improving aim during their white or red grape producing process.

Why can New Zealander every individual white or read grape wine producers improve their white or read grape wine taste more easily? In behavioral economic view, it can explain that why any one New Zealander white or read grape wine producer can be encouraged or excited or persuaded to concentrate nervous and energy and effort to learn how to improve their white or red grape wine products easily.

In fact, New Zealand is one agricultural food export country. It has good natural environment resource , e.g. land, seed to provide any one farmer to produce themselves any kinds of agricultrual food products, e.g. fruit, or wine food products. Because New Zealanders know themselves country has enough natural resource . So, in common, many New Zealanders choose to attempt to do farming agricultural jobs in order to export themselves any kinds of fruit or meat or wine products to overseas or sell to domestic in order to earn profit.

So, when these New Zealand farmers number has been increasing every year. This country farmers will feel themsleves competition between this New Zealand farmers themselves are serious due to they may feel New Zealanders choose to do agriculture businesses in order to export themselves different kinds of farming food to overseas or sell to local to earn profit.

Hence, when many New Zealand farmers feel that farmers number has been increasing every year. They will feel themselves competition is serious. They must need to spend much time and nervous and effort to research what method is the best how to produce the best taste of white or red grape wine products in order to let local or overseas wine buyers to choose to buy his/her producing white or read grpae products to drink.

Hence, in competition psychological view, may influence many New Zealand white or reaad wine producers had been beginning to change their learning behavior on researching what method is the best in order to produce the best quality of taste red or white wine products to sell in order to attract overseas or local white or read grape wine drinkers to choose to buy his/her wine products. Their behavior will focus on learning how to raising or improving white or read grape wine taste method more than only focus on producing a large number white or red grape wine products. They believe wine quality is more important to compare wine producing number.

So, New Zealand wine producers themselves wine producers behaviors have been changing on concentrating on researching wine quality method aspect more then wine producing number aspect in behavioral economic view.

America high technological productive behavior
For America example, US is one high technological country, it owns many high technological knowledge talent inventors, e.g. computer science inventors. Hence, US must attract many diferent countries owning high technological computer inventors choose to go to US to develop their computer science profession career. Also, it seems that when many computer science inventors or professions choose to go to US to develop themselves computer science new career. In behavioral economic view, due to their leaving themselves countries choice, which may bring influence themselve country job behaviors need to be changed. They must need to adapt US new live. Because they will forgive their past computer science job. These computer science professionals need to spend time to adapt US new lives. They " past computer science job behaviors" will need to be changed to their new US any computer employer's new computer science job model.

Because their traditional computer science jobs needed to be forgot in their themselves countries. They will feel their old computer science job knowledge and behavior needed to change in order to let their US any one new of computer company employer feels satisfactory to accept their new working behavior in any one US computer organization.

So, on the other hand, many US computer company employer will feel that they must need time to accept any one new overseas computer science professions their working behaviors, their working attitude daily, because these foreign comouter science professional, their past computer working behaviors and working attitude must be different to US domestic computer science professions.

In behavioral economic view, these overseas computer science professions, their working behaviors and attitude must be needed to change in order to adapt any one US new computer company itself domestic or local computer science professional stafs themselves daily working behaviors and attitude because these overseas and local computer science professionals must need to team work together.

In behavioral economic view, it is only one way that foreign computer science professionals must need to change themselves past country traditiona daily working behaviors and attitude in order to cooperate with these US local computer science professionals in teams more easily.

Consequently, if these foreign compute science professionals can change their past working behaviors and attitude to let any one US local computer science professional feels to cooperate with them easily in short time. Then, the US computer company itself whole computer professional teams themselves efficiencies will be influenced to raised or improved by the changing past working attitude and working behaviors of these foreign computer science professionals. So, in behavioral economic view, only if US any one computer company hopes itself computer teams themselves efficiency can be raised or improved when it decides to employ foreign computer science professionals and US domestic computer science professionals. They need to work in teams together. They must need to let these foreign computer science professionals to know how to change their working behaviors and attitude to let their domestic computer science professionals feel easy to work together. Then, the US computer company itself whole team efficiency must be rasied or improved easily in short time.

● China share market investing behavior

For China share market example, economic development depends on financial market. Because if many Chinese have interest to invest to carry on shares buying and selling activities in orde to learn how to earn shares interest and share profit when the China shareholder can make decision to sell himself/herself shares in the the high price, then he/she can earn money when he/she can sell the China company's shares in the high sale share price position.

If China has many Chinese like to spend time to carry on investing shares activities. Themselves shares buying and selling behaviors will influence China has many companies can increase fund from many Chinese shareholders in order to have enough money to expand or develop themselves businesses in China in long term.

Consequently, when China can have many Chinese like to attempt to carry on buying and selling shares investing behaviors in China share market. Themselves buying and selling shares behaviors can help many Chinese companies have effort to increase enough money or capital in order to continue to do their businesses in long term absolutely. So, it explains why when many Chinese become shareholders , they can assist China will have many companies continue to develop their businesses if many Chinese like to carry on shares buying and selling investing behaviors in long time in

China financial investment market nowadays in behavioral economic view.

Why has any individual country have many people invest share behavior which can influence the country's macro consumption desire?

I shall apply shares market buying and selling investment behavior to explaiin why shares investment behavior which may impact the country's overal consumption desire as below:

In behavioral economic view, I assume that when the coutry has many people have interest to attempt to carry on shares buying and selling investment behavior, then their frequent shares buying and selling behaviors which may bring negactive consumption desire or shopping desire of these shares investors their consumer behavior.

The reason is simple, when the country has many share buyers number suddenly been increasing rapidly. Consequently, these large group share investors must need to spend much time to research any kinds of company shares variations, whether when their share prices will rise up of fall down in order to achieve buying the company's shares in the lowest price and selling the company's shares in the highest price level in order to earn profit.

Basic on this reason, they must need to spend much extra time to research share prices changing behavior every day, e.g. one working person will wait to leave his/her job, after he/she can spend time to gather data to research the day's share price changing behavior after dinner. So, the working person's right time may be his/her share price market research behavior. Before he/she may spend his/her night time to go to shopping after dinner, but nowadays, he/she will fogive to do his/her shopping behavior before dinner or after dinner at hight sometime. He/she will make decision to spend much night time to turn on computer to click on share market website to research his/her share purchase choice to investigate whether his/her share price whether it rises up or falls down at the moment in order to make his/her share buying or selling decision at ever night time.

I mean the when the country has many people are share investors, their shares investment behavioral spenging time which will influence many shops lose customers at might often because the country will have many people feel need to spend night time to turn on computer or watch television to investigate share price variation. So, the country will have many people / share investors choose to stay at home in order to carry on share price variation investigation behavior, they need to listen share market update news from radios or watch the share market update news from computer or TV at home every night. Consequenly, they must reduce times to leave themselves homes at night. So, their shopping behavior also will be reduced. Because these share investors feel need to spend time to investigate share price variation news at homes which can bring economic benefits (high opportunity benefits) when they choose to forgive to leave homes to go to shopping times (opportunity cost) every night.

On conclusion, it seems that when the country has many people are share investors, then their share price investigating behavior may bring negative shopping emotion at night. Consequently, the country's any one shop may lose many customers from this share investor consumer group in behavioral economic view. Hence, when the country's share investors number had been increasing rapidly, it will influence any shops lose many customers from this share investing customer group at night frequenly in short time, even long time in behavioral economic view, because their shopping desires or shopping emotion will be brought negative feeling when they make decisions to spend much time to listen radios or watch TV or computers share price update nes at night. Hence, share market will bring negative impact to influence consumer shopping desire or negative shopping emotion in behavioral economic view.

Can technology influence human shopping behavioral change?
Nowadays, technological development has reached mature stage, whether technological mature stage may bring positive or negative shopping emotion influence to global consumers. I shall aplly internet inventin or ecommerce shopping channel tool to explain whether internet technology can bring postive or negative influence to global consumer behavior in behavioral economic view.

Internet is a good technological tool, it brings e-commerce business chance. In fact, commonly, global has have many businessmen choose to use internet channel to carry on their products transactions between global online-buyers and their electronic websites. So, global many shoppers had begun to feel online shopping is more convenient to compare visiting shops shopping. Their shopping behaviors have been changed from internet technological tool. Global has many shoppers choose to buy any products from any overseas or local businessmen their web stores. They only need to spend time to find any businessmen their webstores to choose the most suitable products to pay visa to buy from their webstores. at homes. So, in general, global had have may shoppers had changed their shopping behaviors from visiting shops to visiting webstores at homes often.

So, it seems that internet technological tool had influenced global many shops disappear, but internet webstores will be replaced their actual shops on streets. Some of businessmen either they choose webstores to replace shops or choose websotes and shops both or still keep shops only. Hence, internet tool influences global businessmen have three kinds of products sale channels to let globa local and overseas consumers to choose how to buy their products.

However, in fact, many of global shoppers, youngers and olders had begun to accept to buy any products from webstores. They feel to spend time to leave homes to visit shops , their shopping behaviors will be wasted time to not essential part to their daily lives. Hence, since internet technological invention, it had changed many consumers their traditional visiting shops shopping habit to change to buying products from webstores channel.

However, on the one hand, internet creates webstores ecommerce shopping channel to let global many consumers do not need to leave homes to go to shopping. It brings negative visiting shops shopping emotion to global general consumers nowadays. But on the other hand, it also brings positive visiting internet webstores shopping emotion to global general consumer nowadays. So, it seems that global many consumers feel that they often do not need to spend much time to go out shopping. Many global consumers feel convenient and enjoy to choose any products to buy from different internet webstores, when the online buyer chooses the most suitable product, he she only needs to pay visa card to buy the product from the online seller's webstore conveniently at home.

Hence, online shopping can bring economic benefit to online buyers, e.g. avoiding walking time or spending transport fare to visit the shop to go to shopping, shortening or reducing shopping time to do another important matter.

On conclusion, global many consumers began feel online shopping can bring more economic benefits on shortening shopping time, avoiding transport fare spending aspect. So, online shopping will be popular shopping behavior for future long time. It may encourage global many shoppers can make rapid shopping decision in short time in order to carry on any products buying transaction to global any one online shopper in short time easily in behavioral economic view. So, global many businessmen had begun to build themselves one attraction webstore in order to persuade different countries consumers to choose to click themselves webstores from internet channel to buy any kinds of products in short time easily.

So, internet technology had changed consumers traditional shopping behaviors to build positive online shopping emotion as well as raise online sellers' any products sale chance easily in behavioral economic view.

Why and how human behavior may influence the country's economic growth or recession?

When one country has many people choose to do the same matter for one period, whether their behavior may influence the country's pvera; economic growth or recession . I shall attempt to indicate cases toexplain their relationship as below:

For flowing rubblish behavioral case example, do you feel that when the country has many people often flow rubblish on the streets, instead of their flowing rubblish behavior may bring streets dirty? But, their flowing rubblish behavior may explain that this country has people may have enough money to buy food to ear, or enough cloths to wear, enough bottles of water to drink, even they may have enough money to buy new television, radio, refrigeraters , washing machines, desktops or laptops electronic home products from old to new to use in order to satisfy their living needs. So, when they flow old electronic home products, their flowing old home electronic products behaviors may seem that they have enough money to buy other new home electronic products to replace old home electronic products to use at homes.

However, it seems thaat this country ought have many people have jobs to do. So, many of them, they can easy to make purchase decison to flow any old home electronic products and buy any new home electronic products to use . Because this country has many people have jobs to do. So, they can often not use old home electonic products to become rubblishs to flow on streets after they had bought any kinds of new home electronic homes.

In fact, it also implies that this country's economy grows rapidly. So, many businesses can glow up rapdly. When they expanded their businesses, they must need to increase employees number in order to let they help themselves to raise productivity or serve their clients absolutely. So, when the country has many businesses can grow up, it seems that its economy must be better or it is improved to compare past. Due to many different kinds of home electronic products had been often bought to use by this country people in this period. So, this country's any streets can be observed that expensive electronic home products were flowed on streets anywhere. then, this country will have many electronic home products sellers can sell their home electronic products very easily. When this country has many people can find any kinds of jobs to do easily. So, due to unemploymen rate had been decreasing.

In behavioral economic view, as this many electronic home products rubblish country case, we can observe this country may have many people have jobs to do. So, consumption number has been increased long time. So, cheap food, or expensive home electronic products may be rubblish on any streets. This country's people , their flowing rubblish behaviors may be explained that many of people have enough jobs to do, so they have ability to buy any good taste food to eat or buy any kinds of expensive electronic home products to use. So, this country's economy may be improved for this long period. So, in behavioral economic view, when this country can have many electronic home products rubblishs are flowed on anywherer in streets frequently. It seems that this country will have many people have jobs to do, so it causes they often change old home electronic products or replaced them easily, when they have enough income to spend to buy any kinds of new home electronic products to use at homes easily. Moreover, their flowing old electronic home products behaviors also indicate that this country has many people their salaries may be increased in possible from their emplyers. When this country can have many different kinds of home electornic products are sold. It means that this country's electronic home products needs or demand had been increasing, due to many people have jobs to do and income increases to excite their living of needs also improve. Consequently, this country may seem have better economic improvement. We can observe from this country's electronic home products rubblish increasing income in theis period.

On conclusion, this country ought experience economic growth at this period. So, " flowing expensive electronic home rubblish increasing number " may seem that this country's economic growth is rapidly in this period, due to many people have jobs to do as well as salaries increase in this period.

Technology how impacts human behavior changing?

Technology how influences human behavior to bring changing? For example, online share purchase and sale transaction from smart phone brings share investor can do share buying or selling transation in any where and any time conveniently, non manual driving auto vehicle, bring car owner feels comfortable and spends free time to do other matter, e.g. reading, listening mucis in himself or herself car freely. electrical energy vehicle can help car owner to reduce air polluton and it can brings the drivers do not feel drive long time in any journeys in order to avoid air pollution for environmental protection responsible car drivers in our societies. Thus, they will drive long time in any journeys when they can drive electronic energy cars to replace oil energy cars.

However, online technology can also bring consumers can choose to stay at homes to buy any things from seller individual online webstore conveniently. Such as online technology can bring shoppers do not need to spend much time to visit shops to buy any things. They can choose any kinds of products from any online sellers individual online webstores conveniently at homes. Online technology excite busy consumers can make purchase decision easily as well as it can help online sellers sell any kinds of products from internet easily.

In behavioral economic view, technology can change human behavior to be improved, it can let human feels comfortable, more free time ro use, rapid making any decisions, such as apply smart phones to make share purchase or sale transaction decision, online shopping decision, even travelling any where decision in short time, when the traveller finds the most cheap hotel accommodation room price and air ticket price frm any travel agent online tourism webstore, then the potential travel customer can follow the online hotel accommodation price and air ticket price data to make decision when to buy the air ticket from the airline travel agent or make decision when to prebook which hotel accommodation room to go to the country to travel from online travel agent tourism webstores. So, technology can encourage global any country travelers to make anywhere to trvel rapidly. If the traveler can find the country's general hotel rooms and airline tickets prices had been decreasing more sightly. The traveler may make travel decision to choose the country to travel in short time, then he/she can prebook the country;s any hotel room and airline ticket to pay by visa fraom the country's any hotel and airline travel agent webstores., before one week, even one month or more easily. Hence, online technology can also encourage traveler individual frequent travel times to be increased, due to global travelers can find any hotel rooms and airline tickets prices from internet conveniently at homes. They do not need to spend time to visit any airline travel agent to enquire travel choice country's hotel rooms prices and airline ticket prices. They can compare global travel of countries choices ' all hotels rooms and airline agents air tickets prices to make prebook airline seat and hotel room decision before one week, one month even six months early.

On conclusion, online technology can encourage global travelers can make travelling any where and when traveling time desicions easily. It can excite tourism industry develops in long time. Also, such as electricity cars invention can encourage environment protection car owners do car purchase decision easily, because they can choose to drive electronic energy cars to replace oil energy cars in order to avoid air pollution occurs easily. So, electronic cars can increase electronic car purchasrs number, due to many of environmental protection attitude of car owners can choose to drive electricity cars to bring air cleans, even non -manual driving cars can encourage lazy driving and free time driving car owners to choose to buy non-manual (artificial intelligent) cars to drive , because they can spend much free time to read, listen music or do any matters in themselves cars, they do not need to drive cars, robotic (AI) auto driving machine is such one non-manual driver to help them to drive themselves cars confidently. So, non-manual driving cars can attract lazy and enjoying free time driving car owners to choose to buy to replace traditional manual cars to drive easily. Moreover, online share transaction can help any share investors to make share buying and selling decision in short time easily. When they can apply smart phones technological tool to carry on share buying and selling activities easily. They can observe any share rising or falling price suitation from smart phones in any where any any time easily. So, smart phone technology can help global any shareholders to make share purchase and sale transaction easily. So, technology can encourage human makes decision in short time rapidly.

How and why employees behaviors may influence economy development?

In behavioral economy view,I believe the country's any organizational employees behavior may bring indirect relationship to influence the country's long term economic development. I shall indicate past manufacture industry social development period to explain their relationship. For many countries' past business activities had belonged to manufacturing industry, such as US, UK past before 1980 year, it focused on steel manufacturing and steel manufacturing related machine products. So, US, Uk developed countries manufacturing industries may be past main country's economic income sources. I assume US , UK past had one million number different kinds of industries. They ought had about seven houndred thousand number organizational businesses were belonged to manufactured industry. They may include:

Steel manufacturing and steel related machine manufacturing, e.g. vehicle manufacturing, home appliances, e.g. washing machine, television, radio, refrigerate cooler, heater, air condition etc. different kinds of different kinds of steel -related manufacturing machine, they were manufactured from US, UK steel machine manufacturers. So, US, Uk the other three hundred thousand number industry may be general service industry, e.g. hotel service, restaurent, cinema, public transport service, tourism lesiure , wine bar, supermarket etc. different kinds of non-manufacturing industries business organizations were operated in UK, US past before 1980 year.

So, in UK, US developed countries industry development history, they ought have high percentage of businesses belonged to steel related manufacturing machine and steel products. Also, in the past before 1980 year, US, Uk business employers , they employed many workers are manufacturing workers. They needed to spend long time to work in factories. They were skillful workers, and they are trained to manufacturing cars, washing machine, television, heater, etc. even steel itself different kinds of steel related products to prepare to deliver to their shops to sell to US, Uk local or overseas clients.

So, I believe that past UK, US ought employ many employees, they belonged to skillful manufacturing workers, manufacture increasing steel machine or steel related machine number of products rapidly daily. So, if UK, US had had many of these manufacturing factories owned high skillful workers, then their manufacturing steel-related machine or steel both kinds of products number must be influenced to raise rapidly. Consequently, their steel machine manufacturing products would been exported to overseas or would been sold to local both markets , they may be influenced to raise sale number. They (these manufacturing workers) needed to be trained to know how to manufactur these different kinds of machine products in the efficient teams and they ought to be trained to raise their efficiencies in order to shorten time to manufacturing many kinds of steel related manufacturing machine or steel itself products rapidly. So , if their efficiencies and manufacturing performance was improved, these US, UK any one manufacturing worker and their teams ought achieve raising productivities significantly.

Hence, when past UK, US manufacturing industry development period, if these two countries' any manufacturing factories could have many manufacturing workers could be trained to be skillful and proficient manufacturing workers. Then, in past every day to these factories workers, they ought help their steel or steel related manufacturing employers to raise any kinds of machine or steel products number in every team. So, when past in the manufacturing industry development, US, UK could have many factories' manufacturing workers themselves steel or steel related machine products manufacturing skill could be trained to to improve to any kinds of these machine or steel manufacuring products quality as well as their products number could be influenced to raise by themselves skillful improvement significantly every day.

Then, what would be influenced to occur to past UK, US manufacturing industry period? In behavioral economic view, when these two manufacturing industry developed countries, such as UK, US , if they had many factories workers can be trained to improve their skill in order to achieve any kinds of steel or steel-related machine products quality could be improved as well as products manufacturing number could be also increased absolutely.

In consequence, past UK and US both countries ought increase themselves any kinds of steel and steel related machine products number to be supplied to themselves local shops to let local clients to choose any one kind of machine manufacturing products to buy easily as well as they could also export to supply overseas any countries to buy their different kinds of steel or steel related machine products to let overseas steel or steel related manufacturing machine product buyers, they can have many of these different kinds of these steel or steel-related different kinds of manufacturing machine from UK and UK these both countries easily to compare other countries.

On conclusion, I believe that past US, and UK macro manufacturing industry income GDP would increase significantly. So, they would have good economic growth performance because when many of these manufacturing workers themselves manufacturing effort could be improved. So, it explained when employees manufacturing abilities can influence economic growth indirectly.

Robots invention whether they can help organizations to raise efficiencies or inefficiencies?

In behavioral economic view, in any organizations, when the organization hopes its worker teams can raise efficiencies , the organization may choose to increase more workers number and/or it can provide training to improve these workets themselves skills in order to raise their efficiencies. For one warehouse example, when the warehouse increases many goods , they are needed to delivered these goods from the shelves to the delivering destination locations. If this warehouse supervisors feel these workers themselves goods delivery speeds are slow, which is possible due to this warehouse's workers number is not enough. So, this warehouse supervisor ought increase workers number in order to increase their goods delivery speed in order to deliver goods from the shelves to every indicated goods delivery destination in order to let any one lorry driver can transport the right kinds of goods and ensure the accurate goods number to transport to any one client home rapidly.

However, if this warehouse supervisor planed to buy several warehouse goods delivery robots to assist these warehouse workers to find the right kinds of goods from shelves and then deliver to the right destination location in the warehouse. So, these warehouse orkers can concentrate on counting the accurate goods number and ensuring the right kinds of goods in order to prepare to let lorry drivers to transport these goods to these goods of buyers themselvers homes rapidly. Consequently, in the first step, robots can concentrate on finding th right goods from shelves and delivers them to the right goods transportation of location destination. Then, in the second step, these warehouse workers can concentrate on counting the accurate goods number and ensuring the right kinds of goods in order to prepare to put them to the lorry. Consequently, when warehouse robots and warehouse workers can cooperate to work together, the most important, robots, can deal on finding the right kinds of goods and deal on delivering the accurate number of goods of job duty as well as these warehouse workers can only concentrte on counting the right kinds of goods number in order to avoid it has none any mistake of wrong kinds of goods and inaccurate goods of delivery number to be transported to the lorry and to deliver to any one buyer's home.

So, it seems that warehouse robots ought help any one warehouse worker to raise himself efficiency and avoid goods delivery of mistake occurrence easily as well as their help to warehouse workers that can let any one goods buyer feels their goods can be delivered to their homes rapidly. Moreover, warehouse robots can also help these warehouse workers to raise efficiencies because warehouse robots can help them to shorten goods delivery time between any one shelf and any one goods delivery destination of location in the warehuse because robots may help them to find the right kinds of goods from the right shelf in the short time. So, any one worker does not need to spend long time to seek anywhere is the right shelf location for the kind of goods when the kind of goods are needed to deliver to the buyer's home from lorry. Warehouse robots can help them to do this aspect of " finding the goods from the right shelf in short time job duty". So, any one warehouse worker only needed tospend less time to do the counting of any right kind of goods number and ensuring the right kind of goods job duty. Consequently, this warehouse 's any one worker, his any one kind of goods delivery time may be reduced, because robots' assistance and they may have more confidence to avoid mistake to deliver the wrong number of goods and/or the wrong kind of goods to any one goods buyer's home.

On conclusion, it seems that warehouse robots ought may help any one warehouse worker to raise efficiency for any one team in the warehouse as well as the warehouse any one supervisor does not need to spend much time to observe any one worker individual performance for " goods delivery job duty aspect" because their goods delivery job duty that had been replaced to do by these several warehouse robots. Robots can achieve the more accurate of right kinds of goods and the right number of goods delviery job performance to compare any one of human warehouse worker themselves right kinds of goods of delivery and right number of goods of delivery job performance. So, when robots can participate to cooperate with this warehouse's any one worker to do their goods of delivery job duty in this warehouse every day. Then, robots can raies any one of supervisor individual confidence in order to let they do not need to spend time to observe any one of worker individual whose goods of delivery job performane. They can concentrate on supervising any one worker whose goods transport to lorry in the final step in order to avoid to deliver wrong goods number and / or wrong kind of goods to any one goods buyer's home every day. Consequently, this warehouse's overall teams of their delviery of goods performance many be improved by robotss' participatin to goods of delivery task as well as this warehouse's oveall teams themselves efficiencies may be influenced to raise by robots' goods of delivery task participation.